Sanctuary of the Sacred Flame

A Guide to Johannite Spiritual Practice

Fr. Anthony Silvia

©MMXIII

In Appreciation

I have come to understand that one does not write a book by oneself, especially when dealing with a topic that is so thoroughly influenced by the people involved in this living and vibrant tradition. I've always felt, when reading other books, that the "acknowledgments" section at the beginning was a bit self indulgent. I could not have been more wrong. I see now why so many people need to receive thanks and praise for their hand in the completion of a book. I am profoundly grateful for all of the people in my life, without whom this book would be nothing more than a check box on a vast to-do list somewhere that I would never get around to finishing.

This book would not have been possible without the support and assistance of my Johannite Family. To all the clergy and laity of the Church who I have had the pleasure to know, your wisdom and experience have helped me to better understand my own spirituality. I have learned so much from you and will continue to do so every day. And to all the Johannites I haven't yet met, I hope this book helps you on your journey, and I look forward to the day when we might break bread together.

To Msgr. Jordan Stratford, who shared his knowledge of the publishing industry and made it seem much less scary to publish my first book. His inspiration and expertise has been invaluable.

To those who volunteered their time and talents to help me edit the manuscript: Msgr. Jordan Stratford, Jill Sophia Fein, Clyde Adams III, Jonathan Stewart, and Msgr. Scott Rassbach. Here's hoping we caught them all!

To Tau Thomas Valentinus, Catholicos of the Alexandrian Gnostic Church. Through many late-night conversations the ideas in this book became more and more refined.

To His Eminence Mar Iohannes IV, whose friendship and support these many years has been a great comfort, and who gave the book a once-over to make sure my foot wasn't too far into my mouth.

To His Grace Mar Thomas, who took a chance on a deacon a few years ago, despite reservations. I hope you haven't been disappointed.

To all of the wonderful people who donated to help

this book get finished. You are each so kind and generous and I truly appreciate the vote of confidence you gave me. Knowing that you were out there and eager to hear what I had to say gave me the strength to finish this book. Thank you!

To all those who contributed prayers and practices for the book. I wanted this to be a reflection of the whole Church, and your contributions helped achieve that.

Most especially this book is dedicated to my parents, without whose constant support this book would not have been remotely possible.

Thank you.

Most Esteemed Donors:

Jeffrey Kupperman

Jonathan Stewart

John DiGilio

Daniel Butler

Scott Rassbach

David Green

Rebecca Dunsdon

Tim Mansfield

Eric Bryant

Marvelyn Davis

Mark Rafferty

Wesley Martusewicz

Daniel Butler

Donald Donato

Jay Moore

Daniel Butler

Gregory Kaminsky

Rosamonde Miller

Gordon Soukoreff (and Todd from Genelle House B&B)

David Sheppard

Jill Sophia Fein

Lance Hoddinott

Foreword by ✠ IOHANNES IV

Practice is essential to being a Gnostic.

Study, reading and reflection are valuable tools, and are vital, but they are vital because they help provide language, context and comprehension to our experiences. Yet, they are neither the source of, nor a replacement for those experiences.

Further to this, intellectual study is important to our journey but the place to which Gnosticism seeks to lead us, dictates that the very thing we understand with, our mind, is in need of transformation as well.

Whether you view Gnostic cosmology as literal, moral or allegorical- the point within the texts is that the entire of our situation is in need of redemption and transformation- this includes the psyche.

Marcel Proust is quoted as saying "The true voyage of discovery lies not in seeking new landscapes but in having new eyes".

Spiritual transformation is not simply about encountering the Kingdom of God, it is also about transforming the very thing that encounters it.

In the Gospels, the word commonly translated as repentance is metanoia ("Beyond Mind") and is not about simply confessing one's errors or ignorance but about transforming the very thing which gives rise to them. This means going beyond our ordinary ideas, thoughts and consciousness- a true change of mind.

As the canonical Gospel of Matthew says "Repent: for the kingdom of heaven is at hand". You will not arrive at the latter, until you arrive at the former.

If a spiritual practice is to be of value, then it must

engage us towards this very transformation.

Father Anthony Silvia's Sanctuary of the Sacred Flame sets out with this goal in mind- to engage the seeker and give them a toolbox to assist in achieving transformation.

This toolbox is not a collection of disparate and discarded items collected off the floor of larger traditions, but a toolbox that is time tested and practice affirmed, informed by both the Johannite tradition and the Christian and Gnostic traditions of which it is a living part.

Even the rituals, practices and approaches unique to the Johannite Church, some of which are made available in this guide, have had the benefit of years of practice by Johannite communities around the globe.

At the same time, these things are neither a static work nor an in stone fixation of practice but a stepping stone to further exploration and inspiration- and as you work with the material provided, new insights, applications and practices will follow. I would not be surprised to see further editions of this work as time goes on, because practice and people evolve together.

This book is a part of the evolution of both Johannite practice and its author, Father Anthony, and it is my hope that it assists you in your own evolution on the Johannite path within and towards the sanctuary of the Sacred Flame.

‡ IOHANNES IV
Sovereign Pontiff and Patriarch
The Apostolic Johannite Church

TABLE OF CONTENTS

Introduction

Chances are you picked up this book in order to learn more about the Apostolic Johannite Church. You may have just found a Johannite parish in your city, or found a reference to the Church on the internet. You're probably wondering what it means to be a Johannite, and this book attempts to give you some ideas about what that might look like. Of course, every person is unique, and there are about as many ways to be a Johannite as there are actual Johannites. We don't see this as a problem to be overcome; rather, it is an opportunity to be embraced. The strength of the Johannite Church is in its diversity. As a result, this book is not intended to be the definitive guide to Johannite practice.

I wrote this as a way to share my take on how Johannites may improve the quality of their personal practice in a manner consistent with the symbols and theology of the AJC. If you have other practices, or if you're feeling creative, please feel free to use these rituals and prayers as an addition to what you're already doing.

The Apostolic Johannite Church is, at the same time,

an ancient and modern expression of Gnosis. Our roots trace back to John the Beloved Disciple and John the Baptist, and and the communities they founded. Our parishes, narthexes[1], and missions operate all over the world, serving people through liturgy, sacrament, pastoral care, education, and community service.

While the overall tone of Johannite tradition is based on the Christian traditions and symbols, you will find members and friends of our Church who are Jews, Muslims, Buddhists, Pagans, "spiritual but not religious," and just about anything else you could think of. There is no inherent contradiction in this. The Church welcomes all who feel that they can identify with our Statement of Principles and who are willing to join with us in paying prayerful respect to the Sacred Flame present in the heart of each person. The details are just window dressing, but at its core the Johannite Church stands unified.

---

1   Narthex is the architectural term that is given to the room at the front of the church, before you enter the sanctuary. We use this term to describe groups that are not yet parishes. They are often led by seminarians on the road to the priesthood.

While participating in the sacraments and educational lectures with a Johannite parish or narthex is usually the easiest and most accessible way to be a part of the Johannite family, this isn't always possible. Ours is still a small church, even though it continues to grow each year, so it may be the case that you live someplace where it would be impossible for you to visit regularly with a Johannite body. This book will give you a place to start. If, after following some of the practices in this book for a while, you feel you would like to try your hand at developing a local Johannite body and providing leadership to such an effort, The book can also point you in the right direction for that.

Even if you belong to a Johannite body already, you might still find this book useful. You don't stop being a Johannite when you leave mass on Sunday. These techniques will give you a foundation for a daily practice that can lead to profound spiritual growth. If you decide not to use the framework I'm about to lay out, I'm sure you'll find at least one or two useful practices in this book to enrich your spiritual practice, regardless of your personal views on theology.

So why bother with all this effort, anyway? Perhaps you think that if you attend mass or lead a moral life then that will be enough. While it's true that those kinds of things are certainly important to any religious practice, Gnosticism has never been a spectator sport. To be a Gnostic means that you actively participate in the work of Salvation. If you're a Johannite then you believe that you contain the Sacred Flame which unites you with the Divine, yet you still exist in a perceived state of separation. It does happen, exceedingly rarely, that Gnosis occurs spontaneously in a person. We could go about our daily lives and hope to be suddenly and unexpectedly Illumined, but it seems inadvisable to sit around and wait while there are things that have been proven to help in the Quest for the Graal[2].

It is my hope that this book will help you advance on the path to Gnosis and beyond. Of course reading a book on spiritual practice is only the beginning; no book can do the work for you. You need to be willing to have discipline

---

2 An ancient French spelling of "Grail" and it is the spelling the AJC uses most often, in order to acknowledge its French roots.

and dedicate yourself to the Sacred Flame. This book offers several tools to start you on the path to Gnosis, if you're willing to put in the time, and I hope you reach it. However, even if you do, Gnosis is only the beginning. The insight that is granted through Gnosis is more like an initiation that allows us to begin the true work of the soul: the pursuit of Theosis.

The descriptions of the practices in this book are brief. This is by design. My hope is that I can give you just enough information to get started in a practice and see if it works for you. I also try to give you the resources to learn more about them so you can go into much more detail with them if you choose to. But this book is about work, not about reading about work, so pick a practice and begin. Real spiritual practice takes a very long time to master, but starting, and trying, and failing, and trying again, is the only way to get there.

What is Gnosis, and why should we practice?

Before we begin we should talk about where we would like to end up. The process of spiritual attainment happens in roughly two stages. The first stage, and the focus of our spiritual practices, is the pursuit of Gnosis, the second is the pursuit of Theosis. This book is about the first stage, as the second stage is deeply personal and cannot be taught or even described well with our frail human intellect. It must be pursued as the result of insights gained through the new state of being granted by the Grace of Gnosis.

So what is Gnosis? It's a Greek word that translates into English as knowledge, but there are a handful of Greek words that are translated as knowledge. The Greek philosophers had some very specific things to say about knowledge, and so they used very specific words for different concepts. Gnosis is different from episteme, for example, another Greek word for knowledge.

When we think about knowledge today in the English speaking world we are generally thinking about episteme.

Episteme is the knowledge of subjects. When you say "I know trigonometry" you are making a claim to have episteme of trigonometry. Gnosis is a knowledge based on experience. "I know my brother" because you have interacted with him and understand him on a fundamental level, and have been fundamentally changed by the experience. Fr. Troy Pierce of the Ecclesia Gnostica describes Gnosis this way:

> We can see echoes of it in notions like 'hands-on experience,' but they fall short. Usually we are reduced to analogies, like the 'difference between knowing the path and walking the path.' Or, 'the map is not the territory.' Some aspects of an eye-witness refer to gnosis, such as recognizing a perpetrator. Yet, the circumstances may limit the process of gnosis, and this has been demonstrated to be susceptible to recognition of the suspect rather than the perpetrator. A better example in the use of gnosis is the practice of having a body identified by the next of kin.

Gnosis, then, in the spiritual sense is an experiential insight into the truth of Divinity, an intimacy with the

Divine. Indeed, through Gnosis you can know the true reality of God. To get there, however, one must have the faith that such knowledge is possible. We have many accounts of Gnosis from both ancient and modern sources, but when one encounters Gnosticism for the first time, a little faith is required to begin down the path.

The idea of faith is often maligned in some modern Gnostic circles, but it's actually a very important part of this process. It's possible that some modern Gnostics find the idea of faith to be distasteful because of the way the word is used in Protestant Christianity. Some Protestant Christian denominations teach that it is faith alone that will "save your soul from damnation." Not so in Gnosticism. Faith opens the door, but it is Gnosis that opens your eyes. Only through Gnosis will we be able to find salvation and Theosis. Think carefully about these words from the Excerpta Ex Theodoto:

> What makes us free is the Gnosis
> of who we were,
> of what we have become;
> of where we were,
> of wherein we have been cast;

of whereto we speed,

of wherefrom we are redeemed;

of what birth truly is,

and of what rebirth truly is.

This, therefore, is the aim of spiritual practice, and the most important goal we can set for ourselves. Our daily lives are constantly giving us reasons to ignore the spiritual dimensions and the true reality of the Divine Fullness. In order to have the Gnosis of who we were and what we have become, we must try constantly to swim against the stream set into motion by the rulers of this world and seek the source. We do this by setting aside time to train our minds to stop reacting to the outside world alone, and to listen for the voice of Holy Wisdom (or Sophia, the Greek word for wisdom and an important figure in Gnostic mythology), whose sole purpose is to lead us back to the Fullness.

We all have to go to work and do our laundry and eat breakfast. There are many things we have to do that come with being a human being in the world, and typically our minds are simply responding to what's going on around us. This isn't a bad thing, but we could be doing so much more. We could be actively participating in the world instead of simply responding to it, and this is a very powerful place to be. Being in this state of mind allows us to clear a space for Divine inspiration to grace us with the Gnosis we seek. It makes a clear path for us to become aware of the Sacred Flame that unites each of us to the Divine. Don't worry, it's not as tough as it sounds. Sophia is always whispering into our ears. All we have to do is train our minds to be able to listen. It doesn't take much.

It's true that spiritual practice is a lot of work, but fortunately you can see the rewards of these techniques here and now. While the ultimate goal is for the soul to enter into the Fullness after death, these practices will provide you with tangible benefits in this life also. When your mind is in a proactive state rather than a reactive one, you will be able to make much more informed decisions about the problems you face. It's no secret that our minds are constantly getting in our own way while we try to make important decisions. Having a clear and open channel for the Divine is the best way to walk through the world making Divinely inspired choices.

The good news is the Divine doesn't want much from

you. Not only that, but you can know exactly what the Divine needs from you through Gnosis. The Divine wants your soul to return to the Fullness. However, this can only happen after your soul is sufficiently prepared in this life by stripping away all of the automatic patterned responses that it has been developing since your birth.

In Gnosticism there is a distinct difference between your body, your soul, and your spirit. Without going into too much boring detail, the spirit, which we call the Sacred Flame, is that part of ourselves that transcends our individuality. You can think of the Sacred Flame as one facet of a gem that intersects with your body and soul. Every other person also contains this Sacred Flame facet, but the gem as a whole is the Divine. It is the awareness, the experiential, intimate, insightful knowledge, the Gnosis of this essential truth that we seek through our practice.

Our soul is that which allows us to interact with the physical world. For most of us the soul is like a mirror. It reflects the world back to itself, but behind the glass is the Sacred Flame. Spiritual practice slowly removes the reflective coating from the glass, allowing the Sacred

Flame to shine through into the world and illuminating everything it shines upon. This is the goal of the Gnostic, and there is nothing more important than this.

How to Know if the Practices Are Working

It's difficult to describe what spiritual attainment looks like, since it is not something that participates in your regular, rational thought processes, but we can use some landmarks to point the way. The aim of spiritual practice is to increase our awareness of the Sacred Flame, so one way of knowing if you're progressing is to notice if you are more aware. This involves a certain amount of discipline in the conscious mind, so many of these exercises will include ways to increase your ability to control your mind more intentionally.

Try this to start with: Find a quiet spot and set a timer for five minutes. Sit comfortably and clear your mind. Just sit there and observe your thoughts for five minutes. Try not to actively think of anything, just pay attention to the words, sounds, and images you experience as you sit. Do that now before you continue reading.

You may have observed a series of random thoughts, or replayed conversations you had today and thought of the things you should have said. Perhaps you thought about your future, dreaming of things you'd like to see happen to you, or things you dread. A song could have been lodged in your head. The chances are you didn't consciously think any of these things. They probably spontaneously popped in there due to some internal or external stimuli outside of your control. This is normal. It's your brain doing what it's been trained to do your entire life. It's the natural state of normal human consciousness, and it serves a certain purpose, though you'll find that it's really doing a lot of unnecessary work for you. These thoughts are what keep you bound to the physical world and prevent you from reaching higher. You can lead a rich and full life in the world, and get all the things done that you need to do, without all that random chatter in there, and, as an added bonus, you will be more open to the things of the Spirit.

Over time as you practice you will find that your thoughts will start to slow down. If you get a song stuck in your head, you'll be able to shut it off once you become aware of it. You'll find yourself with a calm mind much more often. Stray thoughts become fewer and further between. While these things aren't the goal, they are landmarks along the path. Gaining more conscious control of your thoughts is an important step towards Theosis. What happens beyond that is a lot more subjective, and you'd be better off talking with other Johannites about that. This book can get you started, but you'll need to go to the community for more.

Chapter 1: Johannite Basics

In the years after the death of Jesus, there was a community which followed the teachings of John, the Beloved Disciple. John shared the message of the Incarnate Logos, which was the love of God, the love of one's neighbor, and equality before the common Parent of all humanity. This community eventually underwent a split that would see some of them move towards what would become the mainstream Christian Church. Many of them, however, continued to follow the teachings of John, and would go on to become the Gnostics who wrote the Apocryphon of John, among other texts. The secret tradition of the Johannite community continued, often hidden, sometimes inactive, but always present, until the founding of the Church of Christ in France in the early 1800s.

The Apostolic Johannite Church can be described as a modern expression of this Church of Christ1, founded in the early 1800s by a French doctor by the name of Bernard Raymond Fabre-Palaprat. Fabre-Palaprat founded his

Church of Christ after discovering a document that contained, among other things, an alternate translation of the Gospel of John. He was also a Freemason and a member of the Knights Templar, and as such he made some interesting claims about the Gnostic Christian lineage that came from John the Beloved Disciple through the Knights Templar to the modern age. The validity of his claims are virtually impossible to verify, but nevertheless it is from these traditional legends that the modern AJC draws much inspiration.

The modern incarnation of the Johannite church was founded in the year 2000. That early community, then lead by the Most Reverend James Foster (also known by the ecclesiastical title of Mar[3] Iohannes III), collected the Johannite texts and traditions and formed them into a working public church in order to share this important spiritual stream with the world, which, up to this point, had been kept from the public eye.

The AJC can be described as an "esoteric, Gnostic, Christian communion with valid Apostolic Succession,"

3   Mar is a Syriac word that means "my lord." In the AJC it is used to address bishops.

which succinctly sums up the various aspects of the church. The AJC is esoteric[4], in that it values those things that cannot be told, but must be experienced. It is Gnostic, since it is Gnosis that will save us. It is Christian in its sacraments, structure, and its reverence for the Incarnate Logos and the Christian scriptures that tell His story.

At the time of this writing the AJC has parishes, narthexes, and missions throughout North America, Europe, Australia, and New Zealand, and it continues to grow larger each year.

In addition to this brief history, it may also be helpful to define some terms that are used frequently in the Church to describe certain key concepts. The next section will give the definitions of some of the more challenging terms, many of them Greek, that appear throughout Johannite literature.

---

4   From the Greek *esoterikos*, meaning "deeper" or "within"

Some Terms and Definitions

Agape

A Greek word that translates to "love" in English. However, the Greeks have many words for love, all with subtly different meanings. Agape in the Johannite context refers to the love that the Divine has for us, the love we have for the Divine, and the Divine love that we have for our neighbors. This is an important part of Johannite spirituality. It is pronounced "Ah-gah-pay."

Apostolic

Of or relating to the apostles[5]. In the case of the AJC, this indicates that the church can trace its lineage, bishop-by-bishop, all the way back to the apostles. It also indicates that our church belongs to a certain family of churches that do the same. These churches tend to be sacramental in nature, and they usually recognize the validity of the sacraments of the other Apostolic churches, though not always. This can sometimes be tricky and complicated.

---

5   From the Greek *apostolos*, meaning "messenger"

Christ

The word Christ means anointed or consecrated. In the liturgies of the AJC we rarely speak directly about the man Jesus who walked around in the desert some 2000 years ago, but we often speak of the Christ. This isn't to say that the man Jesus isn't important to us. We affirm Jesus to be the Incarnate Christ. However, the Christ is much bigger than any man[6]. The Christ is a living principle active in the world even still, and we can commune with the Christ today through the sacraments, meditation, prayer, ritual, or even going about our normal routine. Every moment is an opportunity to commune with Christ, although some practices make it easier to remember to do so.

Corpus Hermeticum

A series of documents that were used by practitioners of Hermeticism from the 2nd and 3rd centuries CE. They are mostly presented as dialogues in which a teacher, generally identified with Hermes Trismegistus or "thrice-greatest Hermes", enlightens a disciple. The texts discuss

---

6   See the Fifth Principle below.

the nature of the Divine, mind, nature and the cosmos: some touch upon alchemy, astrology and related concepts. Hermeticism is very closely related to Gnosticism and these teachings were very influential in most philosophical and religious thought throughout antiquity.

Esoteric

The word "esoteric" describes something that is not widely understood, or something that has deeper meaning. The AJC uses this word to describe itself because there is a certain amount of mystery that is required in order to preserve the Johannite traditions. It does not mean, however, that we are keeping secrets. All of the sacraments of the Church are open to all people, but they should be approached with an attitude of mystery and awe, for no one can intellectually know the things of the spirit. There is a knowledge of the heart that surpasses all earthly wisdom.

Fullness

The Fullness (Pleroma, in Greek) is the Divine realm of the Spirit. It is the all, and everything is contained within it. In Gnostic cosmology, the Aeons and archons emanate from the Fullness, which results in the creation of the world and all of us. What we perceive as separation from the Fullness is an illusion, one that is dispelled by the Light of Gnosis.

Gnostic

Of or relating to Gnosis. Gnosis is a Greek word meaning "knowledge", but this isn't the kind of knowledge you can get from a book. This is the knowledge brought about by direct experience. It is "I know Jeff," not "I know calculus." Another way to think of it is as a "Divine insight." Gnosis is essential to spiritual development. It opens your eyes to see the world as it really is, and it drives you forward to heal yourself, the rest of humanity, and the whole world. The "G" is silent.

Gnosticism

A specific cultural tradition, characterized by the philosophical and religious ideas as recorded by communities in the Middle East some time before1 though a few centuries after the birth of Jesus. It was first seen in the community of the Sethians, who were originally

Hellenized Jews heavily influenced by the various schools that emerged from Platonism.

With the emergence of Christianity, the majority of these syncretic schools adopted Christian mythography and symbolism, and went on to greatly influence the formation of Christianity itself in its first fledgling centuries. Other early Gnostic movements emerged from with Christianity itself. The four hallmarks of Gnosticism are;

1. a remote Divinity, the Divine Source, known as the Pleroma or the Father, among other names

2. a creation story that details the emanations from that single Divine Source

3. the creation of (or the organization of) a less-than-perfect universe by a creator god who is, also, less-than-perfect in comparison to the Divine Source

4. that knowledge (Gnosis) of this perceived separation from the Divine Source, coupled with the awareness of a part of us that is also Divine, is the key to our salvation

Johannite

It refers to a spiritual tradition carried in part through the initiatory tradition of John the Baptist, exemplified in the relationship between Christ and the Apostle John, brought to fruition in the community addressed by the Gospel of John, the Gospel embraced by early Gnostics, and which, some believe, produced the Book of Revelation and the Apocryphon of John. While some pronounce the "j" sound as a "y" ("Yo-hu-nite"), which is entirely appropriate, most English speaking members of the Church these days pronounce the "j" ("Jo-hu-nite"). Be aware that scholars use the word "Johannine" to refer to the Beloved Disciple and his community. We use the word Johannite to refer to the stream of our tradition as it manifested after that original community dissolved.

Logos

Logos is another Greek word, which can mean a word, saying, speech, discourse, thought, proportion, or ratio. It is the Platonic Ideal; the ultimate essence and underlying reality of a thing, or of all things. It is also the word used in the Gospel of John 1:1 "In the beginning was the word." It is often used to refer to the Christ, but this word is packed with meaning and many fruitful hours of meditation can be spent contemplating its depth. Logos also means "reason" (in the sense of logic) in Greek, which is another potential source of inspiration for our meditations. Pronounced "low-goes."

Nag Hammadi Library

In 1945 a cache of documents was found in the desert near Nag Hammadi, Egypt. This find represents the most complete record of ancient Gnostic thought that has yet been found. Many texts that we will refer to in this book come from the Nag Hammadi Library. You can read many of these documents online at the Gnostic Society Library[7] or you can get a wonderful translation in the book "The Nag Hammadi Scriptures" by Marvin Meyer and James M. Robinson.

Panentheism

Panentheism is a belief system which posits that God

---

7   http://gnosis.org

exists, interpenetrates every part of nature, and timelessly extends beyond it. In other words, everything is God, but God is more than everything. In Gnostic terms, this is the Fullness which emanates the Universe, but there is more than just the Universe.

Soul

The animating principle, one part of the three-part makeup of a human being (Body, Soul, Spirit). It is the Soul which gives us what we call "life." It is also the psyche, our mental and emotional capacities. For almost all people the soul is made up of patterns and programs that we have allowed our subconscious to write since our birth. These patterns are reactions to stimuli and are largely out of our rational control. Spiritual practice works to develop the soul into a vehicle for the divine and bring it under the control of the Logos.

Spirit

That part of us which is Divine. In contrast to the soul, the spirit is eternal and transcendent. When we reject the identification of the self with the psyche and the material world, and instead identify the self as the transcendent Spirit, this is Gnosis.

Theosis

Uniting with divinity or becoming divine. This is the true goal of all Gnostic practice. In Valentinian theology it is the unification of the inner Divine Spark with its corresponding Angel in the Bridal Chamber. It is impossible to describe accurately, since it occurs in the reality of the spirit, but poetic imagery can point to it. The true language of Gnosticism is poetry and art.

Johannite Spirituality and the Statement of Principles

The Johannite Church has a theology that is very specific in some areas but extraordinarily broad in others. We strive to maintain a sense of unity through our sacraments and a few theological points outlined in our Statement of Principles; however, the AJC has preferred an organic unity to a constructed, legislated or enforced uniformity whenever possible.

Johannite spirituality uses the pattern of Christian tradition as a basis for our liturgies and hierarchies. The Gnostic and the Johannite streams specifically travel through the valley of Christianity. It is understandable that some people may feel uncomfortable with high church Christianity, given recent scandals, and the strict dogmas of the Roman Catholic Church especially often lead to strong reactions. This is one reason why the AJC doesn't require any formal membership in the Church in order to take part in our sacraments or other programs. There are many people who attend Mass regularly who don't identify as Christian at all. We're not trying to be all things to all people, but since Gnosis is so intensely personal we've found that the more restrictions that are put into strict dogmas and definitions, the less likely it is for one to be open to the experience of Gnosis.

We will now go into some detail on the Statement of Principles, as it is what really defines us as a church. The Statement of Principles consists of a series of nine affirmations that define the boundaries of the Church. They are intentionally broad so as to allow for many varied expressions of Gnosis, but not too broad that anything goes. Any discussion of the principles, however, will be necessarily incomplete, and these interpretations are merely my own and do not represent any official position of the Church. Each point deserves much contemplation and meditation. I will briefly give some broad ideas for each point, but further research and study by each Johannite is encouraged.

The First Principle

We affirm that there is one Great, Unknowable, and Ineffable Godhead that made manifest the Universe through Emanation and that while the Universe is contained within this Divine Godhead, the Godhead transcends it.

God is one, though we cannot truly understand God using our faculties of rational thinking. If we try to define God we simultaneously define what is not God, which is impossible. There is nothing that is not God. What we know as the physical Universe was created through a process of emanation, and is contained within God. This is similar to some ideas found in the esoteric Jewish tradition known as the Kabbalah. This is also known as panentheism.

The Second Principle

We affirm that every Being contains the 'Sacred Flame,' a Spark of the Divine, and that Awareness of the Sacred Flame within constitutes the highest level of Self-Knowledge and the Experience of God simultaneously. This act of Awareness, which is held to be liberating, transcendent and experiential, is called Gnosis.

This principle is both the definition of Gnosis and the process by which it is achieved. We use the symbolism of the flame in order to convey a sense of wonder, and a little bit of danger, among many other things. Fire is beautiful, it keeps us warm, it cooks our food, but it also destroys the things we hold dear if we're not careful. Many things that we think are essential to who we are will need to burn in the Flame before we can bask in the Light of Gnosis. Notice that the knowledge of one's self, one's true self, and the experience of the Divine occur together, once we are truly aware of that Sacred Flame which unites us with the divinity that is everything and then some.

The Third Principle

We affirm that there are many ways in which Gnosis may be experienced. Thus, we promote freedom of thought in pursuit of one's inward Path towards the Divine, whether that pursuit is modern or ancient in origin, or individual or communal in experience.

What brings you to that awareness of the Sacred Flame may not work for me, and my path may not appeal to you. There are many paths on the mountain, and many lead to the peak. We may travel together or separately, but as long as we travel with love, tolerance and good intention we will be brothers and sisters in the journey.

The Fourth Principle

We affirm that the Godhead is composed of three Persons, which are one in substance – God, the Father Almighty; the Son, the Logos or Christos Sother (Christ the Savior) and the Holy Spirit or Pneuma Hagion.

Johannite Christianity, like our mainstream cousins, is trinitarian. The language we use to refer to the three Persons of the Godhead usually come from traditional sources, though we understand that any words that try to describe the Divine are necessarily imperfect.

The Fifth Principle

We affirm that God guides us towards Unity by the loving example of the Incarnate Christos, manifested in the life of Jesus, and the ongoing experience of the Holy Spirit as the source of continued Inspiration and Revelation via Gnosis.

The man Jesus was the exemplar of our liberation. The Incarnate Christ, in the person of Jesus, showed us the way to become like Him through Gnosis. We believe that the Holy Spirit still inspires people today, and it is through the Grace of the Holy Spirit that we achieve the glorious vision of Gnosis.

The Sixth Principle

We affirm the One, Holy, Catholic and Apostolic Church that is built upon the message and authority of the Incarnate Christos and that the same lives from age to age by the guidance of the Holy Spirit and the stewardship of the Successors of the Apostles.

There is one church of Christ, one body, with many distinct parts. No one individual denomination is the "One True Church," not even ours. The church adapts to the time and place where it finds itself, under the guidance of those who have inherited the mantle of responsibility from those who have come before.

The Seventh Principle

We affirm the Seven Sacraments of the One, Holy, Catholic and Apostolic Church which act with the Holy Spirit and the Sacred Flame within us to promote unity with the Divine and in the community of Believers.

The seven sacraments are Baptism, Confirmation, Matrimony, Penance, Holy Orders, Eucharist, and Unction.

We share these sacraments in common with the other denominations in Christ's church.

The Eighth Principle

We affirm the use of sacred writings that reveal the Divine message of love and compassion throughout history. We especially revere the Christian New Testament, the writings of the Old Testament and others, the Nag Hammadi Library texts and the Corpus Hermeticum as potent sources for this teaching.

Many Christians believe that the canonical Bible is the only text to be revealed to humanity by the Divine. We go a bit further. In addition to the texts listed, we find the work of Divine inspiration in many sources, including modern ones. As seen in the fifth principle, the Holy Spirit continues to inspire whoever is prepared to receive inspiration. However, books were written by people, even the books inspired by the Holy Spirit. Sometimes it can be a challenge to discern the Divinely inspired bit from the everyday writings of the person who wrote them. The ultimate authority is your own heart.

The Ninth Principle

We recognize the Sacred Flame to be present in all Beings and therefore our Offices are open to all humanity without discrimination on the basis of gender, race, social status or sexual orientation.

Every person carries the Sacred Flame within. There are many who are not aware of it, but that does not make them unworthy, only unprepared. You may hear about ancient Gnostic teachers who divided humanity into different "classes" of people (such as the Valentinian division of Hylic, Psychic, and Pneumatic). These are not types of people, but states of being. There are times when each of us are at various states of piety or stages of spiritual development, and these stages are fluid. It is for this reason that any person of sincere aspiration can take part in the sacraments of the Church, without discrimination whatsoever.

Johannite Divine Love Practice

One very important part of Johannite spirituality is the concept of Divine Love, or Agape. We find this concept spelled out in the Gospel of John[8] in Chapter 13, verses 34 and 35:

> "A new commandment I give to you, that you love one another, even as I have loved you, that you also love one another. By this all men will know that you are My disciples, if you have love for one another."

The word used here in the original Greek is Agape. In the original Greek meaning it refers to the love one has for one's family or an activity (I love singing, for example)[9]. We narrow the meaning of Agape even further to refer to Divine Love. It is a kind of unconditional love that we strive to share with others. But love, especially Divine Love, must be experienced to be understood, and

---

8   It appears in the Fourteenth Gospel in the Levitikon, an important document to the Johannite tradition.

9   This is in comparison to "philia," brotherly love, and "eros," sexual love.

so this brings us to our first practice.

In our daily lives we encounter many different people. Some we interact with more than others, like our families, co-workers, or fellow students. Other we don't interact with much at all, like the other people on the streets, waiters at restaurants, clerks at cash registers, and many more. As Johannites we must acknowledge the Sacred Flame to be present in each and every one of them. Sometimes this can be difficult. People will cut you off in traffic. Someone may speak to you unkindly. But you have to remember that the outer mask of personality that you see when you interact with someone is not the most true expression of that person. Each person is, at his or her core, an expression of the Sacred Flame, and if you start to treat them as such, your own outlook will start to change. This is the beginning of a very important step on your spiritual journey.

This practice is very simple but extremely difficult to master. Try to remember, with each person you see every day, to consciously think to yourself "I love you." You don't need to say it out loud, of course, but really project a sense of love to the person, from your heart directly to theirs. You can also try to visualize a Flame burning in each of your hearts, and they each glow a little brighter when you interact. The Sacred Flame is only one, even though it appears to be separate in each of us. By reaffirming that link we have with all of humanity we raise the awareness of all beings. This must be done unconditionally and the goal here is for that feeling to become automatic. Try to remember to share your Divine Love with every person you see. It will cause a profound change in the way you view the world, if you let it.

The Johannite Church in the World

The goal of the Apostolic Johannite Church is to bring people to an awareness of the Sacred Flame within. This is done primarily through the local parish or narthex. A parish is both a geographical area served by the AJC and the people who are served by it. A parish is usually led by an AJC bishop or priest, but can sometimes be led by a deacon or, less frequently, a seminarian in Minor Orders[10]. A narthex is a small group dedicated to study, prayer, and community, and will possibly one day become a parish. It is usually led by a seminarian studying to become a priest, but occasionally a narthex may be led by a lay person more-or-less permanently, if there is a need for a local group but there is nobody with an interest in taking a

10 The sacrament of Holy Orders is divided, in the case of the AJC, into ten orders, five Minor and five Major. The Minor Orders are Cleric, Doorkeeper, Reader, Exorcist, and Acolyte. The Major Orders are Subdeadon, Deacon, Priest, and Bishop, with the additional "Order" of the Patriarch (technically Patriarch is not one of the Orders, but we refer to it as an Order so that there are ten total, for symbolic reasons).

more in-depth role in the Church.

In addition to the formal work done by the parishes, missions, and narthexes of the Church, our clergy and laity are active in many different areas, but always working to help others come to awareness of the Sacred Flame within. We counsel people in need of spiritual guidance, visit the sick and those in prison, and comfort those who have lost loved ones. We serve our communities in their births, marriages, deaths, and other of life's important milestones. We educate, publish, record, and facilitate discussions of Gnostic ideas. We pray, alone and together, for the Wisdom and insight to share the Light of Gnosis with the world. By reading this book and beginning a spiritual practice, you are about to participate in the life of the Church.

Chapter 2: The Service of the Logos

Ritual plays a crucial part in the life of our Church. Aside from our Statement of Principles, our rituals are an important way of maintaining the unity of the Church. A ritual is, to put it far too simply, a set of actions performed for symbolic value, and has been an integral part of human culture since our ancestors climbed down from their trees. Ritual, especially religious ritual, speaks to a part of us that is larger than each of us as individuals. It acts upon our genetic memory and connects us to those who have gone before. Whether a ritual is performed in community or alone in a corner of your living room, we find comfort in repeating the symbolic actions that tie us to our past, while continuing to live in the present and hope for the future. Remember that ritual acts on the subconscious, and by repeating patterns we build new neural pathways. That's why ritual works. By practicing and repeating the ritual we set up patterns that make it easier for us to remember to act in certain ways as we go about our daily life. Gnosis is about awareness, and true awareness is difficult to maintain as we go about our daily lives, but ritual builds subconscious patterns that helps to keep us in a mindful state more often.

The Service of the Logos is, essentially, an abbreviated version of the Johannite Gnostic Mass. It was developed in order to meet the ritual needs of seminarians and narthex leaders. The Service could be used as part of their own personal practice, or it could be part of the communal life of a Johannite group just starting out, before it has its own member of the clergy. It is being made available to you for the same reasons. This is the quintessential Johannite practice for all members of the Church.

The Logos Service is a ritual designed for use by everybody. It provides a solid framework and symbol set for all Johannite practice. I continue to use it as a part of my practice, even though I've been a priest for some time. It's short and easy to memorize, it's very customizable, and it's chock full of wonderful Johannite symbolism. This chapter will give you the text of the Service, explain what's happening during the ritual, and give you the information you'll need to perform the ritual on your own. Later chapters will give you tools to add to the

Service, but for now, simply perform the Service as it is presented in this chapter until you get the hang of it. After you feel comfortable with it, continue reading the next chapters and add parts that you think fit with your personal style.

When you first start using this service it's a good idea to perform this ritual once a day at a consistent time. Performing it in the morning can set a nice tone for your day. Evenings provide an opportunity to reflect and examine your conscience. Most importantly, perform the ritual at a time when you have the best chance to maintain consistency.

If you are leery about committing to the practice every day, and if you don't have the ability to attend a Johannite Mass regularly, just do it on Sundays. Once or twice a week is far better than nothing at all. If you start with once a week, do it that way for a few months and then start doing three days a week for a month or so, then every day. Ambitious Johannites may choose to do three times a day, using it as a sort of Divine Office. If you choose to practice this often, you might need to do a very short version in the afternoon if you are at work or school, but this is certainly admirable. Ultimately any practice is better than no practice, and maintaining awareness can and should happen outside of the context of ritual; but the more often you do ritual, the better your awareness will be.

The Logos Service is easily adapted for either solo or group practice. If you've been using the Service by yourself for some time, you may find yourself in a position to lead a group in the Service at a discussion group or prayer meeting. This can be a wonderful experience, and it's how I started out in the Church. Building community can be very rewarding, and there will be some tips for this towards the end of the book.

Preparing for the Service

In a pinch, you can perform the Logos Service with nothing at all, but since the effectiveness of a ritual improves as more senses are stimulated, I suggest you gather together at least the following items:

- A flat surface to be used as an altar
- A white (preferably linen) cloth
- A comfortable place to sit near the altar
- 1 white pillar candle
- 4 votive candle holders, 1 yellow, 1 red, 1 blue, and 1 green[11]
- 4 votive candles
- Something to light the candles
- The text of the ritual

At its most basic, the Logos Service is very simple. Anything additional you might want to add comes down to personal taste. If you prefer things simple and uncluttered then stick with the basics. If you like things a bit more busy, then there are a number of things you can

11 If you can't find colored candle holders, then you might try substituting the votive candles with candles of the appropriate colors. This can be tricky, however, because colored candles are often scented. If you have to use scented candles, be careful to pick scents that go well together.

add to your ritual space to stimulate the senses.

You might want to include a cross on or near your altar. You could use a plain cross for this purpose, or you could use a crucifix (a cross with the corpus, the body of Jesus, on it) if that symbolism appeals to you. Burning incense is a great way to get your sense of smell involved. Fresh flowers are always appropriate, as are religious images and statues, icons, or inspirational photos. If you would like to include holy water you can often get some at your local Johannite, Roman Catholic, or Orthodox church. There will usually be a large font somewhere near the front of the church for people to take some home for their personal use. You can include just about anything that inspires you, but remember that objects used for rituals are most effective if they are only used for rituals. Don't light your sacred candles if you just want to add a little atmosphere, save those for your rituals only. Patterns and repetition are what you are working towards.

Setting Up Your Space

Any available space will do for your religious practice, and you can make very effective use of many different kinds of spaces with a little creativity. If you feel a strong connection with nature, go outside. If you feel mystical and esoteric, a dark windowless basement room might serve well. If you have the space to set aside permanently a small chapel or ritual chamber then count yourself lucky. Chances are, however, that you will have to find a corner of a room or make use of a multi-purpose space for your practice. This is fine, but keep in mind that there are a different set of challenges if you are using space in a room that you use for some other purpose. Our brains make strong connections to places. For example, if you use your kitchen table as your altar, your subconscious already associates certain emotions with that table. Happy conversations with your loved ones, family arguments, discussions about money troubles, craft projects; you will be forcing your religious practice to share space with all those things in your mind. This is not insurmountable by any means, you just might have to engage more of your senses in the ritual acts in order to make a more lasting impression.

Place your altar in the east of the space if possible, since that is the traditional placement of the altar in many religions, not just Christianity. If you can't get it in the east, don't worry about it, just place it somewhere that makes sense. Drape your altar with a white cloth. Place the candles along the back of the altar (the side furthest away from where you will stand) in the following order, from left to right: yellow, red, white, blue, green. In whatever space you have left on the altar you may choose to place other inspirational items, the text of the service, or holy scriptures. Do not use it to hold your coffee or any other mundane item. The altar is only to be used for the ritual. If you use a kitchen table or other surface that normally serves another purpose, while the altar cloth is on it it is no longer your kitchen table, it is an altar set apart for the service of the Divine. After you put your ritual supplies away it can go back to being your kitchen table.

A taper candle in a candle holder can be lit before the ritual begins so you can to use it to light the archangelic candles and the Sacred Flame candle. Some find that it ruins the mood to use matches or a butane lighter after the ritual has begun. Also be aware that when using incense there is a danger of setting off your smoke alarms. Try to keep your area well ventilated when using incense. Nothing ruins a good meditation more than a blaring alarm all of a sudden. However, it is not recommended to shut off your smoke alarms or taking out the batteries. It's all too easy to forget to turn them back on afterwards. Safety first. If this is a problem for you then perhaps incense isn't a good option at this time. That's okay. Fresh flowers also have pleasant odors that complement the ritual. Be creative and you'll do fine.

The Text of the Service of the Logos for Lay Ministry

(This Service is under copyright by the Apostolic Johannite Church, used with permission)

[In this text the instructions will appear in [brackets] and in italics. Everything not in brackets, excluding section headings, is to be said aloud. If the service is to be used in a group, the group responds where indicated with an "R:" and everyone responds where there is an "All:", otherwise the individual simply recites all the parts.]

Calling of the Quarters

[All stand.]

[Facing east[12], the yellow candle is lit, saying,]

Leader: Hail Raphael, Ruler of Air, Divine Physician.

---

12 Turning to face in the various directions associated with the archangels is optional, but helps to better establish the sacred space, both in your mind, and as a spiritual reality. If you find that spinning around creates logistical problems for your space please feel free to omit that and simply face your altar throughout.

As the breath of the Divine moves over the face of the deep, so do we call upon you to move over the sanctuary of our being, giving voice to our prayer and strength to our journey.

R: Lord of Wind and Storm, we invoke thee!

[Facing south, the red candle is lit, saying,]

Leader: Hail Michael, Ruler of Fire, Divine Guardian, As a pillar of fire guided our ancestors through darkness, so do we call upon you to light our path through the wilderness of ignorance into the Kingdom of Heaven.

R: Lord of Flame and Prince of the Seraphim, we invoke thee!

[Facing west, the blue candle is lit, saying,]

Leader: Hail Gabriel, Ruler of Water, Divine Messenger. As your presence foretold the Incarnation to our mother Mary, so do we call upon you to help us know ourselves as children of the Divine Beloved.

R: Lord of Stream and Ocean, we invoke thee!

[Facing north, the green candle is lit, saying,]

Leader: Hail Uriel, Ruler of Earth, Divine Companion. As you stand guarding the gates of paradise, so do we call upon you to guide us at our last through the portal of that undiscovered country, from which no traveler returns.

R: Lord of Stone and Vale, we invoke thee!

Leader: Master and Lord our God, You have established in heaven the orders and hosts of angels and archangels to minister to Your glory. Grant that the holy angels may enter with us, that together we may serve and glorify Your goodness. For to You belongs all glory, honor, and worship, now and forever and to the ages of ages.

All: United as one sacred communion with those who were and those who will be, we declare this space and our time here to be holy. Together with the Most High we raise a temple of living stones from the myriad with which we have been blessed, both light and dark. As one, we fashion a temple for your power, an altar for its reception and a sanctuary for your people. Amen.

[The white pillar candle is lit, saying,]

Leader: I am come to cast fire on the earth. And what will I, but that it be kindled

All: **From the Portal of Air, To the Portal of Water, From the Portal of Fire, To the Portal of Earth, From the Center of Power, to the encompassing Adamant, Let this Sanctuary be established within the Sacred Flame.**

Meditation

Leader: The One has brought forth the One, then One, and these Three are but One: [sign of the Cross+] the Father, the Word and the Thought.

All: **Amen**

[Meditation, practice or prayer will go here. The group may be seated.]

Leader: May the Peace of God which is beyond all understanding keep our hearts and minds in the knowledge and love of God. This we ask in the name of [sign of the Cross+] the Father, Son, and Holy Spirit.

All: **Amen**

Dismissal

[All stand]

[As the ritual ends, the candles are extinguished, yellow:]

Leader: Hail Raphael, Ruler of Air, Divine Physician. we thank thee for thine attendance and protection here and before thou departest for thine airy realms, we bid thee hail and farewell.

R: Lord of Air, Hail and Farewell!

[Red:]

Leader: Hail Michael, Ruler of Fire, Divine Guardian, We thank thee for thine attendance and protection here and before thou departest for thine fiery realms, we bid thee hail and farewell.

R: Lord of Fire, Hail and Farewell!

[Blue:]

Leader: Hail Gabriel, Ruler of Water, Divine Messenger. We thank thee for thine attendance and protection here and before thou departest for thine watery realms, we bid thee hail and farewell.

R: Lord of Water, Hail and Farewell!

[Green:]

Leader: Hail Uriel, Ruler of Earth, Divine Companion. We thank thee for thine attendance and protection here and before thou departest for thine earthy realms, we bid thee hail and farewell.

R: Lord of Earth, Hail and Farewell!

[The Sacred Flame candle is extinguished.]

Leader: I give thanks to thee! Every soul and heart is lifted up to thee, O undisturbed name, honored with the name 'God' and praised with the name 'Father,' for to everyone and everything comes the fatherly kindness and affection and love and any teaching there may be that is sweet and plain, giving us mind, speech and Gnosis: Mind, so that we may understand thee Speech, so that we may expound thee, Gnosis, so that we may know thee.

All: Thanks be to God.

Explanation of the Text

The text is short and sweet, so it is a great place to begin a spiritual practice. It's also very profound if you treat it with reverence and consistency. It has three parts, the Calling of the Quarters, Meditation, and Dismissal. Each part serves a particular function, and no matter what embellishments you might choose to make, it's important that you maintain this basic structure. A brief explanation will be given of each element of the Service here; but, as with most things in Gnosticism, much benefit can come from meditation on each word or phrase. A lifetime of study can be spent with just this small ritual.

Calling of the Quarters

In this section five candles are lit and we ask four of the archangels for their presence during the ritual. We call the archangels both as witnesses and to protect our sacred space during the ritual. The orders and hosts of angels and archangels have the specific duty to minister to the glory of the Divine, and that makes them particularly eager to assist us when we perform the Johannite rituals.

These four particular archangels come to the Johannite tradition from Hermeticism. The four Greek classical elements are Air, Fire, Water, and Earth. It was their belief that all matter was made up of different combinations of these four elements. Through centuries of observation in the Hermetic and alchemical arts, these four elements are recognized to have a spiritual reality all their own. It is this reality that we call upon in our ritual.

In Hermeticism the use of correspondences is very important. The Hermetic axiom "as above, so below" illustrates this principle. For example, Air corresponds with the intellect, communication, the planet Mercury, the zodiacal sign of Gemini, the Kabbalistic Sephirah Hod, and many, many other things, some of them quite contradictory. This adds much richness to their study. There are many books and websites that go into detail about the Law of Correspondences, the study of which will greatly improve the quality of your Johannite practice, but that is beyond the scope of this book. Air is also represented in the Choirs of Angels by the Archangel

Raphael. Raphael is the healer, and his[13] name in Hebrew means "It is God who heals." It is always appropriate to pray to the archangel Raphael when someone is sick. Raphael is also associated with learning, and in honor of this the Johannite seminary is called the St. Raphael the Archangel Seminary.

Raphael is called first because his station is in the east, and in a traditional church the altar is placed in the east. His color is yellow because of the traditional Hermetic association of Air and the color yellow. All of the archangels follow the Hermetic color scheme associated with their elements.

When lighting the yellow candle it is always helpful to visualize Raphael joining you in the east of your space. You can picture him in yellow robes and holding a sword (for the association of Air with the tarot suit of swords).

---

13 Angels are usually considered either symbolically genderless or androgynous, but the English language being what is is, it would be awkward to try to work around our language's gender biases. Therefore I hope readers will understand that my use of male pronouns for the archangels is simply a matter of expediency.

The more rich and full your visualizations are, while stimulating as many senses as possible, the more effective the ritual will be. Remember that Raphael and the other archangels will be actually present with you in your ritual space, so it is important to treat them with respect. Make sure you won't be disturbed during your practice. They are very forgiving, though, and you shouldn't worry about making them angry (unless you are outright mean or intentionally rude) but keep in mind that you are developing a relationship with beings who will help you on your spiritual path. It is only right to treat them with the reverence and respect to which they are due.

Next you will light the red candle for the Archangel Michael, whose name means "Who is like God?" He is the field commander of the Army of God, leading the army against the dragon in the Book of Revelation. He is associated with passion and Fire, and he can be visualized in red robes and holding a flaming sword or a wand (the tarot suit associated with Fire). Michael's station is in the south of your space.

The blue candle is for the Archangel Gabriel, "God is my Strength." Gabriel is the messenger of the Divine, delivering prophecy and explaining visions. It was he who told Mary that she would soon bear a son who would be the Messiah. Gabriel governs Water and the emotions. Picture him in the west of your space in blue robes, holding a chalice.

Uriel is the Archangel of the earth whose name means "God is my Light." The element Earth is that which governs the mortality of all things, as well as those things pertaining to money. Uriel is sometimes referred to as "the Angel of Death" although he isn't to be feared. It is Uriel who will ultimately bring us to the Fullness. Uriel is stationed in the north, wears green, brown, or black robes, and holds either a coin or a pentacle.

Once all four Archangels are stationed in their respective quarters, we may now call upon the Most High God to guard and defend us during our work. This is now a space outside of time and beyond the physical universe. We are acting now within a space of the Spirit, and the physical world and its concerns are no longer relevant to us. We light the Sacred Flame candle and we recall what Jesus said in the Gospel of Luke: "I am come to cast fire on the earth. And what will I, but that it be kindled?" In this way we remember the Sacred Flame within us and create an external representation of it. This focuses our attention on the work at hand.

The next paragraph creates the final seal to our sanctuary. It reinforces the four quarters and places them within the context of a circle, subtly calling to mind the challenge of Sacred Geometry to "square the circle" and Blaise Pascal's description of the Divine as a circle whose center is nowhere and circumference is everywhere. The Center of Power extends to the encompassing Adamant[14], and the entirety of the sanctuary exists within the Sacred Flame. In this way we see that the Sacred Flame not only lives within us, but beyond us at the same time. Things of the Spirit are often described using such contradictions.

Meditation

The meditation begins with the words that revived the modern Gnostic church in the late 1800s: "The One has brought forth the One, then One, and these Three are but One: the Father, the Word and the Thought." These

---

14 Adamant is a word used in some Gnostic texts to describe the Pleroma, or Fullness.

were the words received by Jules Doinel in a vision that inspired him to restore the Gnostic Church to the world after centuries of repression. This phrase refers to the emanations that were mentioned earlier in the Statement of Principles.

It is this section of the ritual that you will expand upon by including a prayer system, meditation, or contemplative practice of your choice. For now, just say a short prayer in this spot or spend a few minutes in silent meditation. The Lord's Prayer or Hail Mary are good to start with because many people will be at least familiar with them, but anything will do for now. Repeat the prayer a few times if you feel like you need to spend more time. The important thing is just to start. The first few times you perform this Service, do it simply and become comfortable with the words and gestures. This entire process should be cumulative, so don't be tempted to jump into the more complicated stuff until you have most of the Logos Service starting to roll off the tongue. Rote memorization is not required; you can read from the text for as long as you need to. Once you get the pattern down you will be eager to add more.

After the prayer or meditation we ask the Divine to seal the effects of our work in our hearts and minds when we leave our ritual space. This helps us to remember the effects of our practice as we go about our daily lives.

Dismissal

In a ritual sense, the dismissal is the part where we thank the spiritual beings that we called at the beginning and let them know that we are finished. It is only right that we thank the Archangels for their attendance and protection during our ritual. We thank them in the order in which they were called, and we bid them farewell so that they are aware that the ritual is over. They return to their places in the world of Spirit and bring with them the energy they've received from our ritual.

The ritual ends with gratitude to the Most High, honored with the name 'God' and praised with the name 'Father.' We acknowledge the teachings we have experienced and the gifts of understanding, sharing, and knowledge that come to us from the Divine. We can now leave our ritual space and return to the world a little better off than when we began.

How to use the Logos Service for your practice

Once you have become familiar with the ins and outs of the Logos Service by doing it for a few weeks with a simple prayer in the meditation section, it's time to begin adding some more robust practices to our framework. The next several chapters will show you some techniques that have proven to be effective for many Johannites who seek the path to Gnosis. This list is by no means exhaustive. You may find many other techniques and practices on your journey that may work just as well or even better for you, so feel free to try things out. The only rule is to use what works and brings you the Gnosis of the Sacred Flame.

Your chosen practice will go into the Logos Service where indicated in the meditation section. The practices chosen for this book fit rather seamlessly into the Service, as they don't have a lot of other props and equipment to deal with. A good practice to fit into the Logos Service will be fairly uncomplicated. It isn't recommended that you include another ritual in its entirety, as that may create confusion. Especially if the ritual or practice in question has its own set of ritual tools and symbolism that were completely different from those of the Logos Service. That wouldn't make them bad rituals by themselves, but they wouldn't fit smoothly into the Johannite framework.

I know that many of my Johannite brothers and sisters are interested in other faith traditions in addition to Johannite spirituality. Some traditions fit more nicely into the Logos Service framework than others. Since the Johannite Church is a Christian church, many practices from mainstream Christian traditions work well in this context.

Buddhism is another tradition that seems to be always on the periphery of Gnosticism. Practices such as mindfulness meditation and chanting mantras can complement Johannite spirituality. Care should be taken, however, to make a clear distinction between Buddhist and Johannite symbols. They sometimes blend in ways that can be confusing to those who don't have much experience noting the differences.

Judaism intersects nicely with Gnosticism through its Kabbalah traditions. Many modern Gnostics have no trouble flipping back and forth between Gnostic and Kabbalistic terms and symbols. There are many worthwhile practices you can explore through the Kabbalistic schools that could work very well with the Logos Service.

The Sufi tradition of Islam also has a great deal of overlap with Gnosticism. Sufi practice has the same aim as Gnostic practice, but in an Islamic context. The interested student could find a wealth of treasures to explore among the Dervishes.

There are practices from the Hermetic traditions that are a natural fit for the Logos Service. Meditations on the Tarot, planetary or zodiacal influences, or alchemical symbols will bring much Illumination to many of the symbols in the Johannite tradition.

The Neo-Pagan movement, while not specifically Gnostic in itself, its roots lie in the Gnostic and occult revivals of the medieval period and later. Many of the practices of modern Wicca, Druidism, and Shamanism often find a crossover into a Gnostic's practice.

Whatever other tradition you choose to incorporate

into your practice, remember the goal: Gnosis. If you find, after a time, that a practice is not helping you to clear your mind of unwanted thoughts and reactions, you should discontinue it. There are virtually infinite choices out there, and it's not worth wasting your time on a practice that doesn't work simply because the aesthetics of it appeal to you.

Chapter 3: Meditation

None of the practices that follow are in any particular order, and none of them are any better than the others. Choose the right practice for you, and don't be afraid to experiment. These are only basic descriptions of these techniques, because there are entire books and websites devoted to their finer points. Regardless, the information in this book will suffice for you to practice for many years. As for meditation, there are many different styles you can choose from. Here are some that are particularly useful for, and compatible with Johannite practice.

The meditation practices in this section are considered discursive meditation. Discursive meditation is a practice that involves an active mental process, as opposed to the Christian Contemplation techniques in the next section, which are practices that require a passive mental state. They are two tools from the same tool box that accomplish different tasks. A discursive meditation is designed to help you more deeply understand something or learn something by way of experience. These meditations require you to think a little, but mostly they provide a method to open you up to an experience of an idea that your rational mind wouldn't have the tools to understand. These are very powerful techniques and the dedicated practitioner will get tremendous benefit from them.

In western meditation you generally want to be sitting in a straight-backed chair with your feet flat on the ground. You might want to place your hands palms-down on your thighs for a number of reasons, but mostly because it is a powerful form to hold for meditation. It doesn't put any extra strain on any part of the body and you can sit that way comfortably for a very long time. If you are limber enough you might try the traditional lotus position taught in eastern meditation. Some people also like to lie on their backs, but be careful not to fall asleep. Make your own choices about posture, but you should be comfortable enough so that your body won't be the cause of any undue distractions.

Beginning With Meditation

If you've never meditated before, then it's a good idea to start with this simple exercise. This will help get you used to sitting quietly and focusing your mind on something. Pay close attention to when your mind wanders; this will give you an idea of what you might need to work on first. Always set a timer for five minutes and do this meditation daily until you can spend five minutes in distraction-free meditative attention. This will take some time if you are new to meditation, but don't be discouraged. It may sound easy, but it's more challenging than you think.

Pick some small object that you can hold in your hand. Sit comfortably in a quiet place and assume your meditation posture. Spend a minute or two examining the object in detail, then start your timer. Close your eyes and visualize the object in your mind's eye. Picture it in as much detail as possible. What does it look like? How does it feel? Does it have a texture? What does it smell like? What do you imagine it would taste like? Does it make any sounds? Involve as many of your imagination's senses as you can. When you get distracted (and you will) don't be discouraged. Each distraction you become aware of is a new opportunity to train your mind to start responding in the way you want it to. Observe the distraction without emotion and let it pass away as you return to the object in your mind's eye. It's easy to be frustrated by your distraction, but don't be. Each time you notice a distraction and return to your meditation you are reinforcing new patterns in your mind. After five minutes are up, return to your normal waking state.

Five minutes might not seem like a very long time, but most people today have no idea how long five unfilled minutes actually is. You become aware, very quickly, of the vast amount of stimuli we experience every second. If you're new to meditating, chances are five minutes will be a real challenge. Before too long, though, you should be able to get through it without distraction. Once you get to five minutes then you should be ready to give one of the other meditation practices a shot.

Keep in mind that even if you've been meditating for many years, you can always have an off day when you just can't seem to concentrate. This is perfectly normal. Don't try to force it and get frustrated. Go for a walk instead, or bake a pie, or do something to take your mind off of things for a while and try again later. Getting frustrated with yourself while trying to meditate is the best way to make yourself hate it, so don't push it if it's not working for you. If you run into a bad spell where meditating is getting tedious you can give yourself a week off, but make sure to mark it in your calendar so you don't forget and let a month go by without practicing.

Icon Meditation

This style of meditation is very similar to the one described in the "Beginning With Meditation" section, only the object you concentrate on should be a holy icon or some kind of religious object. You could use a traditional icon or a painting of a saint or scene from the holy scriptures. You could also use a crucifix or religious statue.

The goal of this meditation is to embody the essence of the icon or object by fully experiencing both the physical object and the concept that it represents. Let's take, for example, a traditional Orthodox icon of the Theotokos[15]. The icon is painted on wood with gold leaf accents. It depicts Mary holding the infant Jesus in her arms.

Place yourself in a comfortable position for meditation. Breathe deeply for a while and relax your muscles. Let your mind wander around the scene in the

---

15 Greek for "God-Bearer," Mary, the mother of Jesus. You can find many such images online if you don't have access to a physical icon.

icon. What does it feel like to be a mother holding her infant son? Does the baby feel comfortable and safe? What would you feel if you were observing this scene in person? Knowing what you know about the rest of the life of Jesus, what do you feel about this moment and the moments to come? Now think about the icon itself. Why is Mary wearing that particular color? What about Jesus? What other symbols can you see in the icon? Why are they there?

Now take a little time to just sit with the image and try to simply feel the emotions present in the scene. If you begin to think too analytically about it, dismiss those thoughts and return to the feeling of the emotion.

You may find it valuable to repeat this meditation several times. Spend about ten to twenty minutes on this meditation. Do your best to come up with your own questions to explore about the object of your meditation. This technique can be a very effective way to immerse yourself in the living stream of our tradition.

Guided Meditation

Guided meditation is a technique in which you listen to someone describing a series of visualizations while you meditate. These can be either pre-recorded or read aloud by a facilitator. Typically they involve visualizing yourself in a specific location or performing certain actions. At the moment, there aren't many Johannite-specific guided meditations available, but here is one that you can use to start with . You can record this yourself and play it back when you're meditating, but be sure to leave lots of empty space for visualization. This meditation is something that has been embellished from a meditation by Fr. Vincent Hovley, S.J. that was featured during a Johannite Conclave at the Sacred Heart Jesuit Retreat Center in Sedalia, CO.

Close your eyes and relax. Let the tension leave your muscles as you breathe slowly in and out. Imagine yourself in Jerusalem on the night of the Last Supper. The room you're in has a low, horseshoe-shaped table covered in food. Fruits, flat breads, lamb, and wine are spread over it, and thirteen men[16] are reclining on beautifully woven rugs around the outside of the table.

You are reclining at the first position, leaning on your left arm with your legs pointing away from the table. Jesus is reclining directly behind you. You look around the room at your companions, with whom you have traveled for years, learning from the Master and sharing that Knowledge with those who are willing to listen. You are content; sharing the Passover feast with your friends is something you've been looking forward to all year. You sigh contentedly as you lean back to rest your head on Jesus' chest. As you lean against him you can hear his heart beating, and you feel your own heart begin to beat in time with his.

As you sit there, your hearts beating as one, you begin to see a golden white Light emanating from the Sacred Heart of the Master. As it grows you notice that your own heart begins to glow as well. You realize that, although this appears as two distinct Light sources, they are in

---

16 And perhaps also several women. The Bible often leaves out mention of the women in Jesus' community, but there were surely many.

truth only one. The hearts glow and get brighter, eventually filling the entire room. The Light extends yet further, until it encompasses all of Jerusalem, then all of Israel, and eventually the whole Earth. The Earth is bathed in the Uncreated Light of the Divine and shines as a beacon, even brighter than the Sun, throughout the universe.

While you begin to slowly return to your normal consciousness, you know that you must continue to carry the Light with you. Your duty is to carry it to all who are willing to listen, just as those Apostles did 2000 years ago, and as you open your eyes you remind yourself to try to see that Light glowing in the heart of every person on Earth.

Meditation on a Text or Concept

Very often while reading Gnostic texts or thinking about Gnostic theology we find passages or concepts that are difficult to understand, challenging, or even contradictory. This is an indication that we need to spend some time exploring those ideas more deeply. Meditation can be the perfect tool for this. Mystical religious concepts were not meant to be understood by the rational mind alone, so we have tools available to get our rational mind out of the way for a little while so our subconscious can grapple with the problem.

As an example for this meditation, let's take a look at this poem by Valentinus, Summer Harvest:

I see in spirit that all are hung
I know in spirit that all are borne
Flesh hanging from soul
Soul clinging to air
Air hanging from upper atmosphere
Crops rushing forth from the deep
A babe rushing forth from the womb.

Begin your meditation by breaking up the passage into short phrases at each line break. Explore each short phrase in turn. This has been translated into English from the original Greek, so we can think about why each word might have been chosen by the translator. As you think about a phrase, think about what the intent of the phrase might be by itself. Go on to the next phrase and do the same. After you have done that for all phrases, think about the poem as a whole. Then, simply sit quietly for a few minutes and observe whatever new thoughts may occur to you. This is when you may receive some very valuable insight.

You can do this for any text, especially those that are puzzling or challenging when you first read them. The possibilities are endless, and this practice is essential for a deeper understanding of Gnosticism. You would be well served to use this one often.

A good place to start would be the Johannite Statement of Principles found at the beginning of this book. Doing a series of meditations on each principle will help you really understand each essential point of Johannite spirituality. Also, there are far more ancient Gnostic texts available for this practice than you will likely ever have time to do, so there is a wealth of great material out there for this practice. Pick one and meditate on a short piece of it every day until you get through the whole thing. It will require quite a bit of time and dedication, but there is no substitute for it if you really want to understand the ancient Gnostics and what they taught.

The Johannite Rosary

The Johannite Rosary was developed by Monsignor Scott Rassbach, rector of the Rose Croix parish in Portland, OR. It uses a traditional Roman Catholic style rosary that you can find anyplace. In finished form this rosary will have five sets of five mysteries, called: The Personal Mysteries, the Mysteries of St. John, the Luminous Mysteries, the Johannite Mysteries, and the Mysteries of the Apostolic Gnostics. At the time of this writing it is still under development and only the Personal Mysteries are complete, but we thought we should include it so that people can start using it. Keep an eye on the Johannite website or social media for news on this, and other new publications from the Church.

Because this practice contains much of the same language as the Logos Service as part of the Personal Mysteries, it is appropriate to pray the Johannite Rosary without the Logos Service. The purpose of the Rosary is to keep in memory certain principal events in the history of the Church and the mysteries of Gnosis. If this is being performed as a group meditation, the leader will say the portions in bold, and the rest of the group will join in after. If performed alone, the entirety of the text should be read aloud.

(The Johannite Rosary is copyright 2011 by Scott Rassbach, used with permission.)

*[In this text the instructions will appear in [brackets] and in italics. Everything not in brackets, excluding section headings, is to be said aloud. If the service is to be used in a group, everyone responds where there is an "**All:**", otherwise the individual simply recites all the parts.]*

[1) Starting at the Cross, recite the Act of Gnosis:]

Leader:

What makes us free is the Gnosis

All:

of who we were,

of what we have become;

of where we were,

of wherein we have been cast;

of whereto we speed,

of wherefrom we are redeemed;

of what birth truly is,

and of what rebirth truly is

[2) Moving to the First Bead, recite the Our Father]

Leader:

Our Father, who art in heaven,

hallowed be Thy name;

Thy kingdom come;

Thy will be done on earth as it is in heaven.

All:

Give us this day our daily bread;

and forgive us our trespasses

as we forgive those who trespass against us;

and lead us not into temptation;

but deliver us from evil.

For thine is the Kingdom,

and the Power,

and the Glory,

Now and Forever unto the ages of ages.

Amen.

[3) On the next 3 beads, recite the Prayer of St. John:]

Leader:

O blessed Christ,

give me stillness of soul in You.

All:

Let Your mighty calmness reign in me.

Guide me, O Lord of Gentleness,

Lord of Peace.

[4) On the next bead, recite the Trio at the Cross]

Leader:

Mary, Sorrowful and Inviolate Mother

John, Evangelist and Beloved Disciple

Jesus, Slain and Risen Again

All:
Mary, John, Jesus. At the foot of the Cross, and
 Upon the Cross
We remember Christ on the Cross.
We remember the Mourning of Mary.
We remember John and the Daughters of
Jerusalem.
We remember Christ Risen.
Bring us Light.

[5) Announce the first Mystery (See Below), recite its
prayer, and pray the "Our Father".]

[6] Recite the prayer of St. John 10 times, once for each bead, while meditating on the Mystery.]

[7] Recite the Trio at the Cross.]

[8] Repeat 5 - 7 for the Second, Third, Fourth, and Fifth Mysteries.]

[9] After the Prayers of St. John for the Fifth Mystery, one of the following may be said:]

All:
Hail, holy Queen, Mother of Wisdom!
Our life, our sweetness, and our hope!
To thee do we sing, awakened
children of Eve, to thee do we send
up our hope, for wholeness,
compassion and understanding.
Hear your children, most gracious advocate,
and send us sight to see; and
after this our exile show unto us the
blessed fruit of thy holy Logos;
O clement, O loving, O Holy Sophia.
Be with us, O holy Mother of God
And lead us back to our eternal home.

[-or-]

All:
O Divine Logos,

Transform me into Yourself.
May my hands be the hands of Christ.
Grant that every faculty of my body
May serve only to glorify You.
Above all,
Give me sight to see what has always been
The Kingdom of God, without and within
That we may attain to the Holy Gnosis,
and have a share and an inheritance
with all the saints and adepti
who have pleased you since the beginning.
Transform my soul and all its powers
So that my memory, will and affection
May be the memory, will and affections
Of Christ.

[-or-]

All:
Hail Mother
Rightful Queen of faithful souls,
Who never erred,
Who never lied,
Follower of the rightful course,
Who never doubted
lest we should accept death
in the realm of the wrong god;
as we do not belong to this realm
and this realm is not ours -
teach us Your Gnosis

and to love what You love.

The Mysteries:

[For each Mystery, before you begin, you pray the short prayer and then, for each bead, keep the quality listed in mind as you say the prayers.]

The Personal Mysteries:

[The First Mystery: Raphael and the Qualities of the Element of Air:]

Leader:

Saint Raphael, Ruler of Air and Divine Physician. As the breath of the Beloved moved over the face of the deep, so do we call upon you to move over the sanctuary of our being, giving voice to our prayer and strength to our path. Blessed Angel whose name means "God has healed", one of the seven spirits that stand before the Most High, noble and mighty Messenger of God, who guarded your friends from danger, strong helper in time of need, guide and counselor of your people; pray for us.

[These are the qualities of Raphael and the Element of Air.

Meditate on these while you pray the decade:

1. *Air*
2. *Mind*
3. *Healing*
4. *Movement*
5. *Travel*
6. *Knowledge*
7. *Flexibility*
8. *Leniency*
9. *Curiosity*
10. *The Qualities of Air in me]*

[The Second Mystery: Michael and the Qualities of Fire]

Leader:

St. Michael, Ruler of Fire, Defender of Humankind, As our spiritual ancestors didst travel by a pillar of fire through darkness, so do we call upon you to guide us through the desert of the Kenoma into the Kingdom of the Pleroma. Lord of Flame and Prince of the Seraphim, Standing at the right of the altar of Incense, Strength of God, Angel of Peace, Guardian Angel of the Eucharist, Protector of the Sovereign Patriarch, Terror of the evil spirits, Victorious in battle against evil, Guardian and Patron of the Universal Church, pray for us.

[1. Passion
2. Creativity
3. Leadership
4. Enthusiasm
5. Courage
6. Vigor
7. Self-Respect
8. Will
9. Transformation
10. The Qualities of Fire in me.]

[The Third Mystery: Gabriel and the Qualities of Water]

Leader:

Saint Gabriel, Ruler of Water, and Divine Messenger. As the Incarnation of the Logos was foretold to the Theotokos by your presence, so do we call upon you to be with us that we may truly know ourselves as children of the Most High. Lord of the Deep, who stands before the throne of God, model of prayer, peace and light of souls, admirable teacher, first adorer of the Divine Logos, pray for us.

[1. Awareness
2. Tranquility
3. Modesty
4. Devotion
5. Cooperation

6. Adaptation

7. Integration

8. Empathy

9. Reflection

10. The Qualities of Water in me]

[The Fourth Mystery: Uriel and the Qualities of Earth]

Leader:

St. Uriel, Ruler of Earth, Divine Companion. As you stand guarding the gates of paradise, so do we call upon you to lead us at the last through the portal of that undiscovered country, from which no traveler returns. Lord of Stone and Vale, who strengthens the gifts of the Holy Spirit, who uses the sword of truth to pare away all that is false, bringer of Justice, Light of God, Guardian of the oppressed, the unjustly accused, and the suffering, pray for us.

[1. Respect

2. Stability

3. Tenacity

4. Caution

5. Reliability

6. Seriousness

7. Objectivity

8. Practicality

9. Punctuality
10. The Qualities of Earth in me]

[The Fifth Mystery: The Most High and the Qualities of
Spirit]

Leader:

We give thanks to thee! Every heart and mind is lifted
up to thee, oh undisturbed name, honored with the name
God and praised with the name Father, for from thee
comes every fatherly kindness and understanding, and
any teaching there may be that is sweet and plain, giving
us mind, speech, and Gnosis. Mind so that we may
understand thee, speech so that we may expound the,
Gnosis so that we may know thee. Turn your face towards
us, bless us, and pray for us.

[1. The Kingdom
2. The Foundation
3. The Splendor
4. The Victory
5. The Beauty
6. The Severity
7. The Mercy
8. The Understanding
9. The Wisdom
10. The Crown]

Johannite Chakra Meditation

This practice comes from one of our Johannites in New Zealand, Andrew Rockell. It takes the eastern system of the chakras and marries them to the seven "I am" statements in the Gospel of John.

First Phase:

Face the direction of the sun.

Slow your breathing down.

Imagine breathing the rays of the sun into your own body.

After a minute or two, focus your attention on the perineum.

Imagine breathing the light of the sun into the perineum, or the seat of the First Chakra.

Continue until there is a sense of that center coming alight and glowing.

On subsequent breaths, while keeping awareness of that first sphere of light alive, imagine you are stretching the light and breathing the light up into your genital region (Second Chakra). Picture a second sphere of light brightening there.

Keeping both spheres alight, extend the column of light up into the belly (Third Chakra).

With three spheres active, extend the light up into the heart (Fourth Chakra).

Continue up into the throat (Fifth Chakra).

Again on up into the middle of the forehead (Sixth Chakra).

Then again up to the crown of your head (Seventh Chakra).

Finally, extend the light beyond the crown to the idea of a zone about a hand's breadth or so above the head.

Having found this extra sphere, ignite that.

Second Phase:

There should now be the sense of a string of light with eight illuminated spheres rising up through your body.

Having activated them, return your attention to the first sphere.

Breathe into the first sphere again.

Exhale the phrase "I am the true vine."

Release.

Raise attention to the second sphere. Inhale.

Exhale with the phrase "I am the way, the truth and the life."

Release.

Raise attention to the third sphere. Inhale.

Exhale with the phrase "I am the door."

Release.

Raise attention to the fourth sphere. Inhale.

Exhale with the phrase "I am the bread of life."

Release.

Raise attention to the fifth sphere. Inhale.

Exhale with the phrase "I am the good shepherd."

Release.

Raise attention to the sixth sphere. Inhale.

Exhale with the phrase "I am the light of the world."

Release.

Raise attention to the seventh sphere. Inhale.

Exhale with the phrase "I am the resurrection and the life."

Release.

Raise attention to the eighth sphere. Inhale.

Exhale with the phrase "I am the Alpha and the Omega."

Third Phase:

Return and rise through the chakras simply (re)activating each with the brief phrase: "I am."

CHAPTER 4: CHRISTIAN CONTEMPLATION

Christian Contemplation is a series of practices that come to us from the mystical side of some mainstream Christian churches. In Christian Contemplation the aim is to stop all conscious thought and abide in the love of the Divine. It's hard to describe, and these practices are best taught by an experienced teacher, but this chapter will give you a pretty good head start. If you decide that one or more of these practices appeal to you and you'd like to make a more serious effort to delve deeply into them, then you should find a teacher or a group in your area that is working with these techniques. A good place to start would be the Contemplative Outreach organization (contemplativeoutreach.org). They are dedicated to promoting these practices in a nondenominational setting, and chances are they have a group somewhere not too far from you.

Centering Prayer

Centering Prayer is a type of Christian contemplative prayer that has its roots in the Desert Mothers and Fathers of early monasticism, works like "The Cloud of Unknowing" and the writings of St. Teresa of Avila and St. John of the Cross, among others. It rose to popularity in the modern era through the writings of three Trappist monks of St. Joseph's Abbey in Spencer, Massachusetts in the 1970's: Fr. William Meninger, Fr. M. Basil Pennington and Abbot Thomas Keating.

While the practice of Centering Prayer is quite simple, mastering it can take a very long time. The goal of Centering Prayer, as described by Abbot Thomas Keating, is to maintain the will (intention) to "consent to God's presence and action during the time of prayer." Your aim should not be to focus intently on your sacred word, but to arrive at a place of pure intention, or "unknowing" and simply existing in the glow of Divine Love.

It is best to learn Centering Prayer from an experienced teacher, but until you have a chance to do that there is nothing wrong with starting the practice.

The basic steps are as follows:

Sit comfortably with your eyes closed, relax, and quiet yourself. Be in love and faith to God.

Choose a short sacred word that best supports your sincere intention to be in the Lord's presence and open to His divine action within you (e.g. "Logos", "Gnosis," "Fullness," "Sophia," "Aeon," "Divine," "Shalom," "Spirit," "Love," etc.).

Let that word be gently present as a symbol of your sincere intention to be in the Lord's presence and open to His divine action within you. (Thomas Keating advises that the word remain unspoken.)

Whenever you become aware of anything (thoughts, feelings, perceptions, images, associations, etc.), simply return to your sacred word, your anchor.

Do this for 20 minutes, no more. If you feel moved to pray more, add more sessions of the prayer instead of adding length to the prayer. Ideally, the prayer will reach the point where the person is not engaged in their thoughts as they arrive on their stream of consciousness.

This is the "unknowing" referenced in "The Cloud of Unknowing." You will experience many moments when your mind will start to wander. As you become aware of the fact that you are thinking, simply return to the word and let your thoughts go without judgment. One image that may help is to imagine your thoughts as boats traveling down a stream. You are sitting at the bottom of the stream watching the boats drift by without any concern for them. Of course, this is not something you should actively visualize during the prayer, it's simply a good metaphor for the process.

You will be distracted. Distractions are a part of the process. Centering Prayer does its work on the intention. Being distracted gives us a chance to reaffirm our intent to contemplate. If you find yourself distracted by your thoughts 50 times during one session of prayer, that is 50 more times you got to practice returning to silence.

This is a very powerful practice, and it has the added benefit of being very portable. While it's great to do it in the context of your ritual practice at home, it's also great to pull out during a break at work or school. All you need is a quiet place to sit and some uninterrupted time and you can practice Centering Prayer.

For more resources on Centering Prayer I recommend you read "Finding Grace at the Center" by Fr. M. Basil Pennington. There is also a lot of good material on the web at http://contemplativeoutreach.org where you can find resources, retreats, courses, and a directory of local prayer groups that you can join. I also gave a workshop on Centering Prayer at GnosticNYC and you can watch that video on the GnosticNYC YouTube channel: http://youtube.com/gnosticnyc

Lectio Divina

Lectio Divina is Latin for Divine Reading. It is a process of contemplation using sacred scripture as a focus. It, too, has its roots in the practices of the Desert Mothers and Fathers and has been used extensively as part of a Benedictine spirituality. This practice is a very effective way to open yourself to the inspiration of Divine Wisdom. The practice itself can be hard to describe, and, like other practices in this book, if you if you feel particularly drawn to it, there can be no substitute for the interaction with an experienced teacher. However, don't let that prevent you from giving it a try based on these instructions.

As a method of reading and experiencing the scriptures, this practice differs a little bit from the method described earlier for meditating on a text or concept. While the goal of that earlier practice is to gain a more intellectual understanding of a particular text or idea, the goal of Lectio Divina is to simply be open to Divine inspiration in a much more passive and receptive way. Both methods definitely have their uses, and combining the two can be a very meaningful way to approach a text.

The process of Lectio Divina is fourfold; Read, Meditate, Pray, Contemplate.

Read: Pick a short passage from a sacred scripture, typically three or four sentences. The Psalms or the Gospels are good places to start from in the canonical scriptures. The Gospel of Thomas works quite well from the Gnostic perspective. Read the selected passage aloud, slowly. Observe your thoughts on this passage. Pick a word or short phrase that jumps out at you as important. This can be anything. Don't judge the word or phrase, just let Holy Wisdom guide you. Whatever you find interesting, that is your word or phrase.

Meditate: Turn the word or phrase over in your mind gently. Don't simply evaluate the phrase intellectually, but allow your mind to wander over it and try to put yourself into the scene. You are searching for thoughts and insights that arrive spontaneously. If you find your mind wandering, simply acknowledge that fact and return to the word or phrase. As with Centering Prayer, every distraction is another opportunity to train your mind to respond in a way that you want, instead of reacting based on old patterns.

Pray: Take whatever insights you gained and offer a prayer to the Divine. This can be anything. You may be moved to pray for something you discovered in the Meditate phase, for yourself or for someone else. You may be moved to a prayer of praise for the Divine. Keep an open mind and follow your heart. You will find something appropriate when the time comes. This prayer might be in the form of a simple thought or image, it may be a common prayer you already know or a spontaneous utterance from your heart. Anything you do during this stage will be appropriate as long as it comes from a place of honesty and sincerity.

Contemplate: Very similar to the Centering Prayer, the contemplation stage is a time of silence. You sit in silence and allow the insights you gained from your work to be absorbed into your personality. There is an interesting metaphor used to describe this process: Imagine you are eating. Taking a bite of food is like Reading. Chewing the food is like Meditation. Savoring the essence of the food is like Prayer. Digesting the food and making it part of the body is like Contemplation.

Each stage of Lectio Divina can take anywhere from about 2 to 10 minutes. Generally 20 minutes will be enough time for the whole process, but don't get too caught up in the time it takes. You also might find that, for a particular passage, one or more of the stages aren't coming to you. It's fine to skip them. You may also be moved to take the stages in a different order. Follow your heart. All prayer is useful.

You can also use Lectio Divina in a group setting. One person can guide the process while the group contemplates the same scriptural passage. If desired, the individuals can share aloud the word or short phrase they found, and also share any insights they gained, although sharing is optional.

A good place to find more about Lectio Divina would be chapter 13 of "Wisdom Jesus" by Cynthia Bourgeault, which is an excellent book in general, and Cynthia's take on Lectio is terrific. In addition, Bishop Tim Mansfield (then Father Tim) gave a talk on this subject at a recent Conclave. You can watch that video on the Church's

YouTube channel:

http://www.youtube.com/johannitechurch

Hesychasm

Hesychasm, properly, is a series of religious practices that come from the Eastern Orthodox traditions, the aim of which is to provide the hesychast with direct experiential knowledge of the Divine. This goal, although not referred to as such in Orthodox circles, is Gnosis. Traditional hesychast practitioners are careful to make a distinction between the experience of the "Uncreated Light of God" as they call it and Gnosis as the ancient Gnostics understood it. But despite the terms used, both Gnostics and Orthodox use the same practice most effectively.

The practice of hesychasm is complex, but at its heart it is a practice designed to eliminate stray thoughts so that the Uncreated Light of God can shine through the practitioner. This is done by the constant repetition of the Jesus Prayer; "Lord Jesus Christ, Son of God, have mercy on me, a sinner." It's a short and simple prayer, but centuries of tradition in the East have proven it to be most effective.

The prayer is usually prayed while counting on a

prayer rope. The prayer rope is like a rosary of sorts, only made out of wool cord and made up of special knots. Most prayer ropes contain 100 knots, but they may contain any number; it depends on the preference of the hesychast. The prayer is recited aloud for each knot. One hundred prayers takes about 15-20 minutes if you are going at a comfortable pace.

The Jesus Prayer isn't treated like a mantra, you aren't repeating the prayer for the sake of repeating it. The Prayer is a way of training your intent, similar to the Centering Prayer. When you pray your entire attention is focused on the prayer. Each time you repeat the Prayer you are given an opportunity to evaluate your mental state and realign yourself with the Divine through silence. Your mind will wander, distractions will occur, this is part of the process. Simply return to the prayer and to the state of internal silence.

If you are interested in making this your primary practice, a good choice for further reading would be "The Way of a Pilgrim" by an anonymous Russian author. For now, simply start praying, repeat the Prayer 100 times, and maintain your attention on the Prayer. When you are distracted by stray thoughts, just return your attention to the Prayer and continue.

Bishop Thomas Langley of the Alexandrian Gnostic Church gave an excellent lecture on this subject at the Johannite Conclave in 2009, which you can watch the video on the Church's YouTube channel. The bishop gives a very good explanation of how the Prayer works and upon what part of the mind it works.

Chapter 5: The Liturgical Year

Our lives are full of milestones, celebrations, and times of sadness. So too is the life of the Church. We encounter the festivals of the church on a yearly cycle, which makes for a nice rhythm, acknowledging the seasons of the physical world while pointing to the eternal spiritual world. What happens to the body of the Church also happens to us individually, and so as we travel around the wheel of the year we experience the many happy and sad events that occur in the church calendar. As the Hermeticists say, "as above, so below." No matter where you are on Earth, you are not alone when you celebrate the Life of the Church. Because of the communal nature of these festivals, even if you are far away from a Johannite community, you can rest assured in the knowledge that we are all celebrating these events together.

This chapter will detail some of the festivals of the Church calendar and will give you some suggestions for how to celebrate alone or with your fellow Johannites. As with a lot of the practices in this book, some of these practices come from more mainstream Christian traditions, though we give them a Gnostic twist. Others are specifically Johannite. But no matter the original source, they are all appropriate ways for Johannites to celebrate the liturgical seasons.

Of course, if you have an opportunity to attend the Johannite Gnostic Mass with an established parish or mission of the AJC on any of these holidays, that is strongly encouraged. If you are anywhere within a few hours' drive of a Johannite body I would highly recommend making an effort to visit it - at the very least - on the feast days of the two Saints John, as these are especially important holidays in our tradition.

This is only a selection of the holidays in our Church's liturgical calendar. A full list of the holidays of the Church can be found in the appendix. Also, many of these feasts are not fixed calendar dates. The Johannite Church follows the Roman Catholic dating scheme, and many such feast calendars can be found online.

Agape Meal

Before we get into the specific festivals and seasons of the Church, there is a practice that fits in rather well with many of these holidays, and that is the Agape Meal. Very similar to the Logos Service, it serves as a frame for a meal, either with family, friends, or gatherings of Johannites in community. If done in a group setting, the various parts of the Agape Meal ritual can be split up among the participants. In circumstances where the Agape Meal is used the Logos Service is not used.

The Agape Meal can be used for any holiday, special occasion, or for any reason at all, but I find it to be most appropriate at the celebratory holidays. The holidays for the two Saints John, Christmas, Easter, and the fathers of the Church work particularly well for Johannites. The following description of the Agape Meal comes from Bishop Timothy Mansfield, Bishop of New South Wales, Australia:

The Agape Meal is a prayerful feast shared in community. A feast is a time for a whole household to come together and give thanks. It's a semi-formal occasion which happens as a part of everyday life, but is nevertheless marked out as special (think about birthday parties, Thanksgiving dinners, anniversary celebrations, dinner to celebrate a promotion).

Historically, feasts are shared, abundant and hospitable. An Agape can be an excuse to dress up, to invite old friends or new friends, or those who need a break. It is an expression of our recognition of how the Divine's overflowing abundance indwells us as individuals and as a community.

In the life of an AJC community, you can think of an Agape as a bridge. It bridges the domestic, mundane reality of the meal with the sacred time of liturgy – so it has a flavour that is somewhat liturgical and somewhat casual. As the liturgy proclaims: there is no separation between these things – but it's easy to think of sacredness as only being at church or in meditation. Agape is a way to remind ourselves that truly "there is nothing mundane in the holy".

When an Agape is held around dusk it also catches a resonance of a Jewish Shabbat dinner – though there are many differences, we also light candles, we also give thanks over wine and bread.

The first part of an Agape is call to the four archangels and the opening prayer. You can do this in several ways. If the guests are all church regulars or comfortable with prayer, you can do this at the start of the meal; you can even hand out the four prayers to be said by different people. If you want the Agape to seem a little more casual or you want to ease new people in, you and your family or the other hosts can say the Gathering prayers before the guests arrive.

You can use the four archangel candles (typically, these are tea lights in a coloured glass) if you like, or face in the respective compass direction instead or both. You should have at least the white pillar candle lit to symbolise the Sacred Flame. The candles can be set on the dining table, on a side table or around the room in the respective directions.

Once everyone has arrived bring some wine and bread to the table for the Thanksgiving prayers. The host should say these. These prayers are adapted from an early church manual called Didache and they are similar to the prayers said at Shabbat and to the offering prayers said at a Eucharist service when the bread and wine are brought to the altar.

There is no particular need to be fussy about the type of wine or the kind of bread. Grape juice is fine, gluten-free bread is OK. It can be plain bread or sweet bread, but it is best if it is made with wheat. Some groups prefer to drink from a common cup, some prefer to pour separate cups – pay attention to who might be ill and use common sense.

The Gospel of John tells us that the Word was with God in the beginning of all things, so in memory of that, it's good to include some spoken word as a part of the feast. That might be a reading from scripture, poetry, a speech or talk, even a song. It can be edifying, rowdy, funny or sad. You can be as creative as you like.

Once dinner is done and before everyone leaves the table, we say the parting prayer (which is adapted from Didache again). The final prayers to the angels can follow the same pattern as in Gathering – the guests can participate or the hosts can say them after the guests leave.

Having given you encouragement to adapt to people's comfort, I also want to challenge you not to be shy about prayer. Even if your guests might not be used to it, if you treat it as normal and enjoyable, they will most likely enjoy it too.

The Text of the Agape Meal

(This Service is under copyright by the Apostolic Johannite Church, used with permission)

[In this text the instructions will appear in [brackets] and in italics. Everything not in brackets, excluding section headings, is to be said aloud. If the service is to be used in a group, the group responds where indicated with an "R:" and everyone responds where there is an "All:", otherwise the individual simply recites all the parts.]

Gathering

[All stand.]

[Facing east, the yellow candle is lit, saying,]

Leader: Hail Raphael, Ruler of Air, Divine Physician. As the breath of the Divine moves over the face of the deep, so do we call upon you to move over the sanctuary of our being, giving voice to our prayer and strength to our journey.

R: Lord of Wind and Storm, we invoke thee!

[Facing south, the red candle is lit, saying,]

Leader: Hail Michael, Ruler of Fire, Divine Guardian, As a pillar of fire guided our ancestors through darkness, so do we call upon you to light our path through the wilderness of ignorance into the Kingdom of Heaven.

R: Lord of Flame and Prince of the Seraphim, we invoke thee!

[Facing west, the blue candle is lit, saying,]

Leader: Hail Gabriel, Ruler of Water, Divine Messenger. As your presence foretold the Incarnation to our mother Mary, so do we call upon you to help us know ourselves as children of the Divine Beloved.

R: Lord of Stream and Ocean, we invoke thee!

[Facing north, the green candle is lit, saying,]

Leader: Hail Uriel, Ruler of Earth, Divine Companion. As you stand guarding the gates of paradise, so do we call upon you to guide us at our last through the portal of that undiscovered country, from which no traveler returns.

R: Lord of Stone and Vale, we invoke thee!

[The white pillar candle is lit, saying,]

Leader: I am come to cast fire on the earth. And what will I, but that it be kindled.

[Making the sign of the cross, everyone present says,]

All: The One has brought forth the One, then One, and these Three are but One: the +Father, the Word and the Thought. Amen

[All are seated]

Thanksgiving

[Before or just after the meal is set, but before anyone eats, prayers are said over wine and bread.]

[Wine is poured and a cup of wine is raised, saying,]

Leader: We thank Thee, Divine Beloved, for the living vine of our tradition, made known to us through the Holy Logos. To Thee be glory eternal.

[Bread is broken into enough pieces for the group and the plate is raised, saying,]

Leader: We thank Thee, Divine Beloved, for the knowledge of life, made known to us through the

Incarnate Christos. As the scattered wheat is gathered and made into bread, may we be gathered in Wisdom, for Thine is the power and glory eternal.

[The wine and bread are shared. The meal is served.]

The Word

[Words are shared during the meal. Discussion, scripture, poetry, a speech, songs.]

Parting

[Before leaving the table, the following prayer is said,]

Leader: Thou, O Ineffable and Unutterable, art the origin of all things through the Word; In this world, men and women give thanks to Thee for food and drink, But to us Thou gavest freely the food and drink of Spirit: the eternal knowledge of Divine Union through the light and example of Christ.

All: To Thee be glory forever.

Leader: Let Grace come and the illusions of this world pass away. Let those who know, come. Let those who do not, be delivered from ignorance

All: Amen.

[All stand]

[As the gathering ends, the candles are extinguished, yellow:]

Leader: Hail Raphael, Ruler of Air, Divine Physician. we thank thee for thine attendance and protection here and before thou departest for thine airy realms, we bid thee hail and farewell.

R: Lord of Air, Hail and Farewell!

[Red:]

Leader: Hail Michael, Ruler of Fire, Divine Guardian, We thank thee for thine attendance and protection here and before thou departest for thine fiery realms, we bid thee hail and farewell.

R: Lord of Fire, Hail and Farewell!

[Blue:]

Leader: Hail Gabriel, Ruler of Water, Divine Messenger. We thank thee for thine attendance and protection here and before thou departest for thine watery realms, we bid thee hail and farewell.

R: Lord of Water, Hail and Farewell!

[Green:]

Leader: Hail Uriel, Ruler of Earth, Divine Companion. We thank thee for thine attendance and protection here and before thou departest for thine earthy realms, we bid thee hail and farewell.

R: Lord of Earth, Hail and Farewell!

[The Sacred Flame candle is extinguished.]

All: Let us go in Peace and the Knowledge of the Lord. Amen.

Advent

The four Sundays before December 25

The Advent season is the period leading up to Christmas. It includes four Sundays and it is a period of preparation. In the Roman Catholic tradition the use of an Advent wreath is employed to mark the time spent in hopeful anticipation for the coming of the Logos at Christmas. The wreath has four candles around the outside, traditionally three purple and one rose, though four white or four purple are also sometimes used, which are lit starting each Sunday of Advent. The rose candle is lit on the third Sunday, while the purple are lit on the other Sundays. There is often a white candle in the middle that is lit on Christmas. This could very well be the white candle used in the Agape Meal if you use that ritual for your Christmas dinner. It is customary to light the candles each night at dinner while a member of the family offers an appropriate prayer. Here are some suggestions.

On the Saturday before Advent:

Divine Beloved, look with the eyes of your love upon this wreath and bless it, which we offer as a reminder of

Your eternal Fullness, without beginning or end. In your mercy keep us free from confusion and protect us from ignorance as we wait in joyful hope for the manifestation of the Redeemer. For You so loved the world that you sent your only Son so that He might bring us to unity with You in the the Fullness. Keep our hearts and minds in the knowledge and love of God, and bless us. We ask this through the Most Holy Logos.

The first week of Advent:

Divine Beloved, we place our hopes in You. We hope for Your return in the hearts of those who follow Your example. Be near to Your people and hear our prayer. Help us to remember the teaching of the Word: "Beloved, now are we the sons of God, and it doth not yet appear what we shall be: but we know that, when he shall appear, we shall be like him; for we shall see him as he is. And every man that hath this hope in him purifieth himself, even as he is pure." Grant us your Wisdom, that we might learn the true meaning of Your Word. We ask this through the Most Holy Logos.

The second week of Advent:

Divine Beloved, we partake in the fullness of Your love. We share that love with each person, knowing that we all carry the Sacred Flame within us. Be near to Your people and hear our prayer. Help us to remember the teaching of the Word: "A new commandment I give unto you, That ye love one another; as I have loved you, that ye also love one another. By this shall all men know that ye are my disciples, if ye have love one to another." Grant us your Wisdom, that we might learn the true meaning of Your Word. We ask this through the Most Holy Logos.

The third week of Advent:

Divine Beloved, we rejoice in You. We celebrate with Your whole church the coming of the Logos. Be near to Your people and hear our prayer. Help us to remember the teaching of the Word: "A woman when she is in travail hath sorrow, because her hour is come: but as soon as she is delivered of the child, she remembereth no more the anguish, for joy that a man is born into the world. And ye now therefore have sorrow: but I will see you again, and your heart shall rejoice, and your joy no man taketh from you." Grant us your Wisdom, that we might learn the true meaning of Your Word. We ask this through the Most Holy Logos.

The fourth week of Advent:

Divine Beloved, give us stillness of soul in You. Grant us your peace so that we might make straight the way of the Lord. Be near to Your people and hear our prayer. Help us to remember the teaching of the Word: "These things I have spoken unto you, that in me ye might have peace. In the world ye shall have tribulation: but be of good cheer; I have overcome the world." Grant us your Wisdom, that we might learn the true meaning of Your Word. We ask this through the Most Holy Logos.

Christmas Day and Christmastide[17]:

Divine Beloved, we give thanks to You for sending the Divine Light into the darkness of our ignorance. Now we behold Him and we shall walk the earth illumined by the

---

17 Christmastide, also known as the twelve days of Christmas, is the period between Christmas and the night before Epiphany.

Sacred Flame. Therefore, let us in our lives manifest the Light within which has been granted to us. Help us always to remember that material things are to be used, and people to be cherished; and that immorality is made manifest when people are used, and material things cherished. We ask this through the Most Holy Logos.

Nativity of the Divine Light, or Christmas

December 25th

Christmas Day celebrates the coming of the Logos to the world. The Word made flesh, the Divine Light whose example was sent to us by the Father so that we might all achieve the Gnosis of the true reality of the Pleroma. On this day we celebrate the coming of the Christ into the hearts of those who follow His example. We celebrate the memory of His first coming, and pray for Him to return in each of us.

Many of us already have some rituals and traditions surrounding the Christmas season. Giving gifts and spending time with family are wonderful ways to celebrate the Nativity, but beware the dangers of materialism. Christmas gifts should be offerings of love, not obligations brought about through guilt.

If your family is willing, consider including the Agape Meal ritual in your Christmas dinner. Centering Prayer is very nice on Christmas, and Lectio Divina focusing on the Biblical accounts of the birth of Jesus are particularly worthwhile. There are also many Gnostic texts from the Nag Hammadi library and other sources that speak about the coming of the Logos, or the Autogenes, or the Christ, depending on the source. In all of the Gnostic creation myths there is always a savior figure sent by the Fullness to redeem the fallen Sparks of the Divine. This is the Nativity story, but in a different form than the one we're used to. Much fruitful meditation can be spent contemplating this concept. If at all possible, it is desirable to attend a Eucharistic Liturgy on this important feast day.

The 12 days after Christmas are properly called the Christmas season, the period leading up to Christmas being Advent. You've heard the Christmas song "The Twelve Days of Christmas"? This is what it is referring to. This period is called Christmastide in some traditions. Special prayers or ritual performed on each of these 12 days of Christmas, with a focus on the coming of the Divine Light, both to the world and into our hearts, would be a great way to celebrate this season.

Holy Apostle John, The Beloved

December 27th

Of course, as the Church of John, this feast is of supreme importance to us. We Johannites ascribe to St. John the foundation of the Secret Church which would become the modern AJC. As we read in the Gospel of John, during the crucifixion, "When Jesus therefore saw his mother, and the disciple standing by, whom he loved, he saith unto his mother, Woman, behold thy son! Then saith he to the disciple, Behold thy mother! And from that hour that disciple took her unto his own home." In this act, Jesus makes the Beloved Disciple, in effect, His brother. So we are all called to be the brothers and sisters of the Christos each day. This is a day, in particular, to acknowledge and celebrate this responsibility.

The first members of Fabré-Palaprat's Church of Christ and his Templar Order were Freemasons. As a result our Church has a historical affinity with Freemasonry, so much so that, at the time of this writing, most of the male clergy in the Church are also Freemasons. The Masonic symbol of the circle with two parallel lines has bearing on this feast and that of St. John the Baptist.

Freemasonry is dedicated to the two Sts. John of Jerusalem, meaning John the Beloved Disciple and John the Baptist. In Masonic tradition the two Sts. John are represented by a circle with a dot in the center and bordered on each side by two vertical lines. It is no coincidence that these two feast days occur in close proximity to the summer and winter solstices, those times when the poles of the Earth line up with the center of our solar system. Those lines on either side of the circle point to this symbolism.

The Sts. John find their feasts on polar opposite sides of the calendar, and represent a much older tradition of seasonal festivals. It is wise to remember this when we celebrate our liturgical year. Our lives are intimately tied up with the world in which we find ourselves. Of course, many Gnostics have a generally negative attitude towards the world, but the AJC doesn't take such a hard stance on that. Matter and the world are the tools we have in order to transcend the world. It's a mystery, and worthy of meditation.

This is certainly a feast where the Agape Meal is appropriate. If at all possible, it is desirable to attend a Eucharistic Liturgy on this important feast day.

Epiphany

January 6th

Epiphany is a complicated holiday. It commemorates a number of different events in the life of Jesus, and, by extension, our lives and the life of the Church. Most notably in the western churches it is a celebration of the visit of the Magi to the newborn Jesus. The Eastern Orthodox also celebrate on this day Jesus' baptism in the River Jordan by John the Baptist. It is also traditionally the day of the miracle at the wedding at Cana, an important story in John's Gospel. For the Valentinians this is one of the most important festivals of the liturgical calendar, perhaps more important than Christmas and Easter. The timing of Epiphany is worth mentioning as well. It falls on the 13th day after Christmas, immediately following the 12 days of Christmas, or Christmastide, and marks the official end of the Christmas season.

Epiphany is also the day when homes are blessed by the parish priest or a member of the family in many traditions. Blessing a home can provide a certain unexplainable peace, and serves to set your home apart as a safe place where the forces of the Demiurge and his minions will have more difficulty intruding. It's tempting to view things of the spirit as metaphors or as representations of psychological processes. Both of these views have value, to a point, but there are spiritual realities that exist beyond the physical world, and we partake in those realities through the Sacred Flame. Blessing is one bridge between the world and the Pleroma.

At the Epiphany mass the priest will bless special chalk that is used to make an inscription of protection over the front door of the home, or all of the outer doors if one is feeling ambitious. For this ritual of blessing you will need some of this blessed chalk and holy water. You can write to your closest Johannite parish to obtain the blessed chalk or email the author (the email address can be found on the Johannite web page) and every effort will be made to get some to you. Holy water can be found in any local Roman Catholic or Orthodox church, usually in a font by the front door. This is made available for the use of the people, so you should not feel uncomfortable taking some home with you. The text of the ritual follows.

Blessing of the Home

[This blessing of the home and inscription of the current year and the initials of the three Magi above each door can be performed either by a priest or a member of the household. This is traditionally done each year at Epiphany, though it may be performed at other times if the need arises.]

[On entering the home,]

Leader (Priest, if present) : + Peace be to this house.

All: + And to all who dwell herein.

All: From the east came the Magi to Bethlehem to adore the Lord; and opening their treasures they offered precious gifts: gold for the great King, incense for the true God, and myrrh in symbol of His sacrifice.

[During the Magnificat (the following prayer), the room is sprinkled with holy water and incensed. After this is completed,]

All:
My soul glorifies the Lord,
my spirit rejoices in God, my Saviour.
He looks on his servant in her lowliness;
henceforth all ages will call me blessed.
The Almighty works marvels for me.

Holy his name!
His mercy is from age to age,
on those who fear him.
He puts forth his arm in strength
and scatters the proud-hearted.
He casts the mighty from their thrones
and raises the lowly.
He fills the starving with good things,
sends the rich away empty.
He protects Israel, his servant,
remembering his mercy,
the mercy promised to our fathers,
to Abraham and his sons for ever.

All: From the east came the Magi to Bethlehem to adore the Lord; and opening their treasures they offered precious gifts: gold for the great King, incense for the true God, and myrrh in symbol of His sacrifice.

Leader: Our Father,
who art in heaven,
Hallowed be Thy name;
Thy Kingdom come;
Thy Will be done
On earth as it is in Heaven.
Give us this day
Our daily bread;
And forgive us our trespasses
As we forgive those who trespass against us;

And lead us not into temptation,

All: But deliver us from evil. For the +Kingdom, thePower, and the Glory are yours, now and forever.

Leader: All they from the east shall come

All: Bringing gold and frankincense and myrrh.

Leader: O Lord, hear my prayer.

All: And let my cry come to You.

Leader: Let us pray. O God, who by the guidance of a star didst on this day manifest Thine only-begotten Logos to the world, mercifully grant that we may attain to the Holy Gnosis. Through the Most Holy Logos.

All: Amen.

Leader: Be illumined, be illumined, O Jerusalem, for thy light is come, and the glory of the Lord is risen upon thee.

All: And we shall walk the earth illumined by the Sacred Flame, and behold the glory of the Logos.

Leader: Let us pray. Bless, O Lord God almighty, this home, that in it there may be health, purity, the strength of victory, humility, goodness and mercy, the fulfillment of Thy law, the thanksgiving to God the Father and to the Word and to the Thought. And may this blessing remain upon this home and upon all who dwell herein. Through the Most Holy Logos.

All: Amen.

[After the prayers of the blessing are recited, each room of the home is sprinkled with holy water and incensed. The current year and the initials of the Magi (traditionally Caspar, Melchior, and Balthasar) are inscribed upon the doors with the blessed chalk. (The initials, C, M, B, can also be interpreted as the Latin phrase "Christus mansionem benedicat" which means "Christ bless this house".)

Example: 20 + C + M + B + 14

The inscription may be written using the blessed chalk without any of the accompanying ritual, though the full ritual is, of course, ideal.

An alternative inscription can be used, including a counting from the date of the Era of Gnosis Restored (1890), and appears thus: 2014 + C + M + B + 124]

Bernard Raymond Fabré-Palaprat

February 18th

Father Donald Donato, translator of the Levitikon and Rector of St. Sarah's Parish in Boston, has this to say about Dr. Fabré-Palaprat:

> Dr. Bernard-Raymond Fabré-Palaprat was born in the town of Cordes in 1773, which is in the historical province of Languedoc, in southwestern France. The nearest prefecture to Cordes is the city of Albi, namesake of the Albigensians: the Cathars. In addition to being a medical doctor to the Court of Napoleon I, he was a high-ranking member of the Grand Orient de France (the Grand Lodge of French Freemasons), and Grand Master of the Order of the Temple. For his service to his country the citizens of the city of Paris, in 1814 he was awarded the rank Chevalier in the Legion of Honor, France's highest order of merit. Later in life, Fabré-Palaprat was appointed to the Société Galvanique of the Academy of Sciences, which was responsible for identifying and rewarding the best

and brightest scientific minds in France, particularly in the quest for understanding and harnessing electricity.

According to some accounts, he brought the Templar order out of hiding in 1804 after it was suppressed by the Roman Pontiff and the King of France in 1307. Shortly thereafter he discovered a document in a used bookstall in Paris called the Levitikon, was comprised of a synopsis of the doctrine and ecclesiastical code of the Johannite Church, in addition to commentaries on the Gospel of John, The Revelation (Apocalypse) of John, and the first public appearance of Gospels According to the Primitive Church - a slightly different version of the Gospel of John. Fabré-Palaprat used this document to institute (or re-institute) the Johannite Church and make it the official church of the Knights Templar. It is this tradition that we follow today, not exactly in the form that Fabré-Palaprat established - a lot has changed in 200 years - but the modern AJC is definitely the spiritual successor to Fabré-Palaprat's church.

The Agape Meal is a good practice for this holiday, as are meditations on the Statement of Principles of the

Johannite Church.

Lent

About 6 weeks before Easter, Ash Wednesday to Maundy Thursday

The Lenten season is a time of preparation for the resurrection of the Logos. This is particularly important for Johannites and Gnostics in general. As the Gospel of Philip says: "Those who say that the Lord died first and (then) rose up are in error, for he rose up first and (then) died." and "Those who say they will die first and then rise are in error. If they do not first receive the resurrection while they live, when they die they will receive nothing." As you can see, the resurrection of the Logos is an example for us to follow in our own lives. The preparation for our resurrection while alive is an important part of what this book is all about.

Fasting is traditional for Lent. Either the full Eastern Orthodox fast can be observed, or a more mild Roman Catholic fast can be used instead. The traditional Roman Catholic fast (at least in North America) is fairly simple: No meat (fish is allowed) on Ash Wednesday and Fridays during Lent. Those with a stricter observance will also limit their meals to only one large meal on those fast days, with maybe one or two small snacks during the day if needed. While not explicitly mentioned most of the time, junk foods and sugary snacks are generally contrary to the spirit of the fast and should also be avoided.

Some Roman Catholics also have a practice of "giving something up" for Lent. A devout Roman Catholic will stop doing something he or she loves to serve as a reminder of the season and its meaning. For example, an avid coffee drinker may give up coffee, or one might give up sweets for the entire season. There are endless possibilities. You may also consider including this tradition with your fasting routine.

Easter

The Sunday following the full moon on or after March 21st.

Easter is a time of celebration in the Johannite Church. We celebrate the resurrection of the Logos, an event with many possible esoteric interpretations. The mainstream churches understand this to be the day when the man Jesus rose from the dead and began to give more teachings to his disciples. This is certainly one valid way of experiencing Easter, but another, more esoteric understanding is this: As the Christ sacrificed himself on the cross of matter in order that He might teach us by his example, so the resurrection reflects our ultimate state of reintegration into the Fullness. The Christ's victory over death is his teaching, helping us to achieve the resurrection in this life. As the Gospel of Philip tells us: "In this world, there is good and evil. Its good things are not good, and its evil things not evil. But there is evil after this world which is truly evil - what is called 'the middle'. It is death. While we are in this world, it is fitting for us to acquire the resurrection, so that when we strip off the flesh, we may be found in rest and not walk in the middle.

For many go astray on the way."

Gatherings with family and the Agape Meal are a perfect way to celebrate Easter. If at all possible, it is desirable to attend a Eucharistic Liturgy on this important feast day. You can also include this Easter prayer by John J. DiGilio, a Johannite seminarian from Chicago:

A Gnostic Easter Prayer

Blessed Christos,
Most holy and most high.
Divine Word incarnate in human flesh,
You endured a life of hardship,
And yet lived a life of love.
Grant that we might learn,
From your humble example.
Emanation of the Divine Unknowable,
You suffered most grievously.
You were scourged willingly,
That we might know the truth
Of our own existence and suffering.
You bore witness to Divine promise,
That very promise that is our own.
Your blood shed and your body broken,
That our birthright would be illuminated.

We now bear witness to your grace,
And are moved by your selflessness.
Our eyes are opened by your sacrifice.
In you, we see the Divine Light,
The flame that burns within us all.
We glorify your holy name.
We venerate your most holy passion.
We give you thanks and praise.
Miserere nobis. Alleluia! Amen.

Pentecost

Seven weeks after Easter

Pentecost celebrates the outpouring of the Holy Spirit upon the eleven apostles and several disciples after the death of Jesus. It is marked as the beginning of the Christian church, because at that moment the followers of Jesus received the Grace to minister to the people. Because of this it is the tradition of the Johannite Church to have its annual Conclave near to Pentecost.

As we read in the book of Acts, the Holy Spirit was accompanied by the sound of "a rushing mighty wind" as tongues of flame settled upon the heads of the early mothers and fathers of the Church. In honor of these symbols celebrations of Pentecost are usually accompanied by brass ensembles, lots of candles, and the color red. Consider decorating your altar with red fabrics, candles, and flowers while you perform the Logos Service on Pentecost. Also read the story from the book of Acts, chapter 2, which describes the first Christian Pentecost.

Always remember that being a member of the one, only, holy catholic and apostolic church means that you have a duty to those around you. Remember to use your gifts of the Holy Spirit for the good of others. As the Logos said in the Gospel of Thomas: "What you will hear with your ear proclaim from your rooftops. For no one lights a lamp and puts it under a bushel, nor does he put it in a hidden place. Rather, he puts it on a lampstand, so that everyone who comes in and goes out will see its light."

Nativity of St. John the Baptist

June 24th

Our tradition holds that the Johannite community has its origins in the community of St. John the Baptist. Indeed, John the Beloved Disciple was a follower of the Baptist before Jesus' public ministry. As such, we owe a great deal to the Baptist and his community. See also the entry for St. John the Beloved for more information about the timing of the two saints' feast days.

The Mandaeans - the world's oldest surviving Gnostic sect - revere John the Baptist as their Messiah. Their tradition appears to be a continuation of the work of John the Baptist. Since parts of the community of the Beloved Disciple would go on to become the first Christian Gnostics, it stands to reason that another community related to the Baptist would find its way to Gnosticism as well.

Courageous Johannites might consider including locusts and honey with their Agape Meal for this feast. For those less courageous, simply including honey is a fitting tribute. There are also many interesting icons of the

Baptist that would be wonderful for Icon Meditation.

Holy Mary Magdalene

July 22nd

According to the Gospel of Philip, Mary Magdalene was called the companion of Jesus. In recent years much speculation has been made of this in works of fiction, and I will leave the interpretation of that up to you, but Mary Magdalene has always been an extremely important figure in the Gnostic traditions. In the Gospel of Mary, she is portrayed as someone who has learned additional teachings from Jesus, which she then shares with the other apostles. She is the first to encounter the resurrected Jesus in the canonical Bible, and as a result she is known in the mainstream church as the apostle to the apostles. Theologians in both the mainstream Christian and Gnostic traditions now reject her characterization as a prostitute, believing that to be based on a poor understanding of the Bible. However, much wisdom can be found in contemplation of the stories told of her in both the Biblical and Gnostic source texts, and an accurate reading of what the ancient world actually thought of her can bear much fruit.

Restoration Day

September 22nd[18]

This is the day we commemorate the restoration of the modern Gnostic Church. Jules Doinel, a French archivist, Freemason, and Spiritist had a vision in 1888 in which he was consecrated by the Aeon Jesus and two Bogomil bishops, and was commanded to restore the Gnostic church. He did this on September 21st in 1890, which he proclaimed to be the first year of the Era of Gnosis Restored.

This has been a very controversial event in the history of the modern Gnostic Church, since the original consecration came to Doinel during a Spiritist séance. However, spiritual revelation has always been controversial to some of the more literal-minded. The history of Doinel's Church and his legacy is extremely interesting, including schisms, allegations of devil worship, and fraud. I would encourage any Johannite

18 In reality the date of the Restoration is September 21st, but the Church was already celebrating the feast of the Holy Apostle Matthew on that date, so we shift it back one day.

interested in church history to study this era in particular.

Our church does have lines of succession that come from Doinel's Church, but they are not considered our primary lineage. Lineage is another interesting topic of research for those so inclined. Since the Church is transmitted through time by way of individuals, lineage holds a certain importance to us. Not nearly as important as the work of the Church in the world today, but interesting nonetheless. We acknowledge our spiritual ancestors and the gifts they gave us from times past, and Doinel was an important part of that tradition.

Use of the Agape Meal would be very appropriate on this day, as would any kind of visionary practice. Scrying, spirit communication, or meditation would all be good ways to honor the day as well.

Chapter 6: Prayers

This chapter specifically refers to prayers that are vocal, a recitation of words, either spoken aloud or recited silently in the mind. There are infinite prayers to choose from in your practice. Prayers could be formal, written down or memorized; or they could be spontaneous utterances from your heart.

Prayer isn't for the Divine; God doesn't need us to pray. Prayer is for our benefit, and prayer is important to a healthy spiritual life. There are be many different subjects of prayer; including prayers for assistance, thanksgiving, praise, and so on. It's important to include many different types of prayer to lead a balanced prayer life. If all of our time in prayer is spent asking for Divine guidance or assistance (a habit into which one can easily slip, especially if one only prays sporadically, and not on a regular schedule) then our prayer life is out of balance. We need to be sure to include thanksgiving, praise, and statements of faith in order to approach our religious practice in a well-rounded manner.

Prayer is a conversation. When you open your heart

to pray, you put yourself in a receptive state. In this state you can listen for the inspiration of the Divine. This can take the form of meditation in a formal sense, or simply sitting in silence. This inspiration can take many forms, and consistent prayer has many benefits. Prayer brings you peace, it clears your mind and helps you think. This is the Divine inspiration, but it doesn't stop there. As with all of the practices in this book, prayer can lead to Gnosis. Prayer is the cornerstone of spiritual practice.

Some Prayers for Certain Occasions

Here is a very small selection of formal prayers you might like to use in various parts of the rituals and practices throughout this book. You could also write your own as the spirit moves you. The prayers that were written by living people have all been included with permission from the respective authors, who retain the rights to them.

Prayer of Solitary Gnostic

by John J. DiGilio

Come dear lady, bring thy light.
For I am lost in the darkness.
In the arms of Archons, I lay.
Their grasp is cold, but firm.
Their promises empty, but tempting.
Come, oh most noble Sophia.
Enliven, yet again, this wavering soul.
For I am so far from our home,
And the path is so uncertain.
Set straight these rambling feet,
And fixeth forth this wandering gaze,
That I may again behold
That oneness that is ours.
That unknowable completeness,

Which exists beyond this world,
Beyond thy pristine bridal chamber.
Come dear, dear lady,
and bring again thy light.

Falconress Prayer

From the AJC's Sophianic Eucharist

Holy +Sophia, Daughter of Light, render of the veil, Mother, Spirit, and Presence, deliver us from ignorance, and bring us through Your Grace into our Reunion. Let loose our jesses that we may return to You our Falconress.

Short Prayer for Healing

Most High God, If it be Thy Will, send forth Thy Holy Archangel Raphael to be with [NAME] and heal [him/her]. Let the experience of this [illness/injury] bring [NAME] and [his/her] family and friends closer to You. We ask this through the Most Holy Logos.

Prayer of St. Augustine

Late have I loved you, O Beauty ever ancient, ever new, late have I loved you! You were within me, but I was outside, and it was there that I searched for you. In my ignorance I plunged into the lovely things which you created. You were with me, but I was not with you. Created things kept me from you; yet if they had not been in you they would have not been at all. You called, you shouted, and you broke through my deafness. You flashed, you shone, and you dispelled my blindness. You breathed your fragrance on me; I drew in breath and now I pant for you. I have tasted you, now I hunger and thirst for more. You touched me, and I burned for your peace.

Prayer of St. Francis

Lord, make me an instrument of your peace,
Where there is hatred, let me sow love;
Where there is injury, pardon;
Where there is doubt, faith;
Where there is despair, hope;
Where there is darkness, light;
Where there is sadness, joy.

O Divine Master,
grant that I may not so much seek to be consoled, as
to console;
to be understood, as to understand;
to be loved, as to love.
For it is in giving that we receive.
It is in pardoning that we are pardoned,
and it is in dying that we are born to Eternal Life.
Amen.

The Thirteen Repentances of Sophia

The Pistis Sophia, an ancient Gnostic text, contains 13 passages known as repentances of Sophia. Some Johannites like to use these as a litany of sorts, reciting each repentance while lighting a candle for each one. These are a bit long, and doing all 13 in one sitting can take a bit of time, so plan accordingly if you plan to do them all at once. You could also make a 13 day devotional out of it. The text of the Pistis Sophia can be found in many places online, but my recommended source is the Gnostic Society Library at http://gnosis.org. The Repentances start in chapter 32. Look for the green text in the left column for the section headings.

Litany of the Holy Archangels

By Michael Strojan

(This is designed as a group prayer, but it would be just as effective for the solitary practitioner.)

Leader: Lord, have mercy on us.
Response: Lord have mercy on us.
Leader: Christ, have mercy on us.
Response: Christ have mercy on us.
Leader: Lord, have mercy on us.
Response: Lord, have mercy on us.
Leader: Christ, hear us.
Response: Christ, hear us.
Leader: Christ, graciously hear us.
Response: Christ, graciously hear us.
Leader: God the Father of heaven,
Response: have mercy on us.
Leader: God the Son, Redeemer of the world,
Response: have mercy on us.
Leader: God the Holy Ghost,
Response: have mercy on us.
Leader: Holy Trinity, one God,
Response: have mercy on us.

Leader: Holy Wisdom,
Response: Pray for us.
Leader: Holy Bride of the Word made manifest,

Response: Pray for us.

Leader: Holy mediator between us and the Word,

Response: Pray for us.

Leader: Holy Raphael, Archangel of the Most High,

Response: Pray for us.

Leader: Holy Raphael, guardian of the rising light,

Response: Pray for us.

Leader: Holy Raphael, guardian of the whirling air and storms,

Response: Pray for us.

Leader: Holy Raphael, Divine physician,

Response: Pray for us.

Leader: Holy Raphael, terror of demons,

Response: Pray for us.

Leader: Holy Raphael, guide of travelers,

Response: Pray for us.

Leader: Holy Raphael, sure guide in the paths of virtue and sanctification,

Response: Pray for us.

Leader: Holy Raphael, whom the Scriptures praise: Raphael, the holy angel of the Lord, was sent to cure,

Response: Pray for us.

Leader: Saint Raphael, our advocate,

Response: Pray for us.

Leader: Holy Michael, Archangel of the Most High,

Response: Pray for us.

Leader: Holy Michael, guardian of the increasing

light,

Response: Pray for us.

Leader: Holy Michael, guardian of fire and leader of the Hosts of Heaven,

Response: Pray for us.

Leader: Holy Michael, standard-bearer of God's armies,

Response: Pray for us.

Leader: Holy Michael, defender of those who hope in God,

Response: Pray for us.

Leader: Holy Michael, standing at the right of the Altar of Incense,

Response: Pray for us.

Leader: Holy Michael, thrust into Hell the eternal Adversary,

Response: Pray for us.

Leader: Holy Gabriel, Archangel of the Most High,

Response: Pray for us.

Leader: Holy Gabriel, guardian of the descending light,

Response: Pray for us.

Leader: Holy Gabriel, guardian of the watery depths,

Response: Pray for us.

Leader: Holy Gabriel, ambassador of the Lord,

Response: Pray for us.

Leader: Holy Gabriel, first adorer of the Divine Word,

Response: Pray for us.

Leader: Holy Gabriel, who foretold the greatness of the Christ,

Response: Pray for us.

Leader: Holy Gabriel, whom the Scriptures praise as the angel sent by God to the Theotokos,

Response: Pray for us.

Leader: Holy Uriel, Archangel of the Most High,

Response: Pray for us.

Leader: Holy Uriel, guardian of the returning light,

Response: Pray for us.

Leader: Holy Uriel, guardian of the Gates of Paradise,

Response: Pray for us.

Leader: Holy Uriel, who brings all at last unto the Heavenly City,

Response: Pray for us.

Leader: Holy Uriel, companion of those who lay down their lives in defense of others,

Response: Pray for us.

Leader: Holy Uriel, bringer of light to those experiencing interior darkness,

Response: Pray for us.

Leader: Holy Uriel, who plants the germ of the Sacred Flame in the hearts of all,

Response: Pray for us.

Leader: Holy Guardian Angel,

Response: Be our constant guide and companion.

Leader: Holy Guardian Angel,

Response: Intercede on our behalf to God the Father,
Leader: Holy Guardian Angel,
Response: Spare us from fear and need and want, now and at the hour of our deaths.

Leader: From all evil, O Lord,
Response: Deliver us, O Lord
Leader: From all sin and occasion of sin,
Response: Deliver us, O Lord
Leader: From anger, and hatred, and every evil will,
Response: Deliver us, O Lord
Leader: From attachment, fear, and delusion,
Response: Deliver us, O Lord
Leader: From the chains and snares of the archons,
Response: Deliver us, O Lord
Leader: From lightning and tempest,
Response: Deliver us, O Lord
Leader: From the scourge of earthquakes,
Response: Deliver us, O Lord
Leader: From plague, famine and war,
Response: Deliver us, O Lord
Leader: By the mystery of Thy Emanation,
Response: Deliver us, O Lord
Leader: Through Thy coming forth into being,
Response: Deliver us, O Lord
Leader: Through Thy incarnation into the world of matter,
Response: Deliver us, O Lord

Leader: Through Thy Christening and Fasting in the desert,

Response: Deliver us, O Lord

Leader: Through Thy triumph over the cross of the elements,

Response: Deliver us, O Lord

Leader: Through Thy holy Resurrection and Ascension,

Response: Deliver us, O Lord

Leader: Through Thy Sacred Union in the Bridal Chamber,

Response: Deliver us, O Lord

Leader: Through the descent of the Holy Spirit,

Response: Deliver us, O Lord

Leader: Through the manifestation of the Sacred Flame,

Response: Deliver us, O Lord

Leader: Holy Lord,

Response: have mercy on us

Leader: Holy and Mighty One,

Response: have mercy on us

Leader: Holy and Immortal,

Response: have mercy on us.

Leader: [Our Father inaudibly] And lead us not into temptation

Response: but deliver us from evil.

Leader: We give thanks to You! Every soul and heart is lifted up to You, undisturbed name, honored with the name 'God' and praised with the name 'Father', for to everyone and everything comes the parental kindness and affection and love, and any teaching there may be that is sweet and plain, giving us mind, speech, and knowledge: mind, so that we may understand You, speech, so that we may expound You, knowledge, so that we may know You. We rejoice, having been illuminated by Your knowledge. We rejoice because You have shown us Yourself. We rejoice because while we were in the body, You have made us divine through Your knowledge.

Response: The thanksgiving of one who attains to You is one thing: that we know You. We have known You, intellectual light. Life of life, we have known You. Womb of every creature, we have known You. Womb pregnant with the nature of the Father, we have known You. Eternal permanence of the begetting Father, thus have we worshiped Your goodness. There is one petition that we ask: we would be preserved in knowledge. And there is one protection that we desire: that we not stumble in this kind of life.

Leader: Let us bless the Lord.
Response: Thanks be to God.

The Divine Office

In some more mainstream Christian traditions there is a set of prayers that are the traditional practices of clergy and monastics, known as the Divine Office, or the Liturgy of the Hours. These prayers are often found in a volume known as a Breviary. The Divine Office is recited in, usually, three to seven sets of prayers at specific times throughout the day. The prayers consist of hymns, psalms, and scriptural passages that vary with the liturgical season of the church.

At the time of this writing, the Johannite Church is in development of its own Divine Office. Once a workable version is ready it will be made available to those who wish to use it. In the meantime, however, until a more permanent Divine Office for the AJC has been established, "A Gnostic Book of Hours" by June Singer is readily available in many bookstores and online and works as a fantastic substitute.

One could also use the Logos Service as a framework for a Divine Office as well. Include a rotation of hymns, psalms and readings and you can put together a serviceable Office. It takes a little work to set something like that up, however, so be prepared to spend some time in research if you choose to do so. If you do, please email the author and share what you've developed. Remember not to hide your light under a basket.

CHAPTER 7: ADVANCED SPIRITUAL WORK

Now that you've seen some practices that are easy to start, let's talk about some things that are a bit more difficult. Some Johannites may be looking for some more intense spiritual work to add to their practice, and the following examples are certainly more intense in that they involve a more serious commitment in order to have a spiritual benefit. It should be pointed out that the practices previously given are as effective as any of these more advanced systems if approached with reverence and diligence. It is simply a question of style. One practice or another may be perfect for you at a given time, and as you progress you may find that you need something more involved. These are all good choices if you find yourself in that situation.

Asceticism

Gnostics identify the self with something transcendent. The self is the True Spirit, the Sacred Flame, the Spark of the Divine. Our bodies, our minds, and even our souls (at least part of the soul, depending on which system you use) are not who we are. Therefore, ascetic spiritual practices are used to discipline the body in order that we may see the True Spirit shine through our physical bodies.

In the west we have come to understand the word "ascetic" to refer to practices or a lifestyle that is very harsh, full of self-discipline. We think of ascetics as individuals who live in caves, wearing rough clothing and flogging themselves while begging God to forgive their sins. While this would certainly fall under the definition of asceticism, the actual meaning of the word is far broader and more interesting.

Asceticism is, simply put, the practice of self-discipline for spiritual gain. In this sense all of the practices in this book are ascetic. Sure, you could be watching TV and eating ice cream, but instead you are denying yourself those things and praying instead. If we look to the Greek origins of the word we can discover an even deeper meaning. In Greek the word has connotations of exercise and training for sporting events. In the same way that you would go to an experienced trainer and develop an exercise routine before attempting to compete in the pole vault, so too should you seek advice from those who have traveled the path before you, and develop a spiritual practice in order to achieve Gnosis of the Divine. Yes, it's possible for someone self-taught, with no formal training, to achieve at the pole vault, but they will never get back the time wasted on trial and error. How much more important is your spiritual wellbeing?

However, in keeping with a more widely-agreed-upon definition, I'd like to share some ideas for ascetic practices that you might want to consider adding to your spiritual routines. Self-discipline can include just about anything, and here is an opportunity for you to be creative with your practice. But be warned, self-discipline for the sake of self-discipline is profoundly unhelpful, maybe even harmful to your spiritual advancement. Asceticism can quite easily be perverted into egotism. For example, using a fast as a way to show the world how pious you are is exactly the opposite of the reason for the fast in the first place. A general rule for ascetic practice is if your practice serves to keep your heart and mind in the Knowledge and Love of the Divine, then it is effective. If, when you sit down to a meal during a fast, you think about the reason for the fast first and the logistics of the fast second, then you are in a good frame of mind. Prayer helps a great deal. If you are sure to include prayer during times of fasting it will place your heart squarely in the presence of the Divine, which is where you want to be all the time.

There are no "mandatory" ascetic practices as part of the Johannite tradition. Johannites aren't ever expected to fast, practice sexual abstinence, simple living, or any other practice. One of the most important principles of the Church is its insistence that your spiritual practice should be your own. Let this chapter be a starting point for you. Take what works for you right now and come back to it later when you want to try something more challenging. Be careful not to over-extend yourself, however. Your asceticism should pose a challenge to you, but if you place yourself in a situation where the fasting or abstinence is simply unfeasible then all of your hard work and planning will be for nothing.

Fasting

To look more closely at fasting, specifically, we will start with some of the traditional methods of fasting practiced in the west today. In the Roman Catholic tradition the most notable example is during Lent, as was detailed in the previous chapter concerning Lent. If you are new to fasting, The Roman Catholic Lenten fast is a relatively painless way to get into it.

The Eastern Orthodox church has a very complicated system of fasting, so I won't give it in excruciating detail; but there is much information readily available on the internet for those who are interested. The following is a basic overview of the Orthodox fast:

In general, fasting means abstaining from meat and meat products, dairy and dairy products, eggs, fish, olive oil, and wine. Wine and oil--and, less frequently, fish--are allowed on certain feast days when they happen to fall on a day of fasting; but animal products and dairy are forbidden on fast days, with the exception of "Cheese Fare" week which precedes Great Lent, during which dairy products are allowed. Wine and oil are usually also allowed on Saturdays and Sundays during periods of fast.

There are four major periods of fasting in the Orthodox liturgical year. The Nativity Fast (Advent or "Winter Lent") which is the 40 days preceding the Nativity of Christ (Christmas), beginning on November 15 and running through December 24. This fast becomes more severe after December 20, and Christmas Eve is observed as a strict fast day. Great Lent which consists of the 6 weeks (40 Days) preceding Palm Sunday, and Great Week (Holy Week) which precedes Pascha (Easter). The Apostles' Fast which varies in length from 8 days to 6 weeks. It begins on the Monday following All Saints Sunday (the first Sunday after Pentecost) and extends to the Feast of Saints Peter and Paul on June 29. The Dormition Fast, a two-week long Fast preceding the Dormition of the Theotokos (repose of The Virgin Mary), lasting from August 1 through August 15.

As you can see, the rules are quite complicated, but this is a very powerful practice. Those who choose this method would be well served to find an Orthodoxy expert to assist them with the logistics of the fasting days and the specific dietary requirements. The Orthodox fast is part of the tradition of the Alexandrian Gnostic Church (http://alexandriangnosticchurch.net), a church in close amity with the Johannite Church. If you are interested in exploring this fast in a Gnostic context, they will have some sound advice for you.

One way to apply fasting to the Johannite tradition is by fasting on those specifically Johannite or Gnostic holidays that commemorate the death or martyrdom of a Templar or Gnostic saint. One could fast for the Cathar martyrs on Montsegur Day on March 16th, for Jaques de Molay on March 18th, for Tau Harmonius on March 22nd, for the Martyrdom of the Holy Templars on October 13th and every Friday the 13th that occurs during the year.

Fasting on those holidays serves to remind you of those who have contributed substantially to our tradition and honors them. It also adds value to your experience of these holidays to try to embody the qualities they represent, both through their lives, spent and given for the Glory of the Divine, and their lasting impact on the modern Church. Meditation on these people and their lives, combined with a fast to honor them, gives one tremendous insight into the ways the Gnosis has presented itself in the world over the years, in a way we can imitate and participate in each day.

Remember, a fast serves to remind us several times during the day of our spiritual commitment. Every time you prepare a special meal or feel a pang of hunger you think about the Divine. This may seem like an extreme way to remind yourself of the Sacred Flame within you, but the Demiurge and his minions (however you view them) are trying very hard to make you believe that this world is all there is. The tools of the world are all we have available to us in order to escape the Matrix (to use a different metaphor).

Also worth noting is that the coin of fasting has another side, feasting. Remember to always end your long-term fast with an appropriate feast using the Agape Meal and celebrating with your family, friends, and fellow Johannites.

Living Simply

Religious life, for many centuries, has included a vow of poverty as one of its primary hallmarks. Monks and nuns of many traditions have followed the Bible's admonition to sell all of of their possessions, give the money to the poor, and live a communal life with those who have also done likewise. While there is tremendous spiritual benefit that can be received from this, very few people are in a position to do it. Most of us have families to support and bills to pay.

This does not mean that we can't participate in a life of simplicity. As Gnostics especially we are called to be in the world but not of the world, which means that we live our lives with the understanding that the true reality of the Divine is far beyond the things of our world, and the things of our world just aren't as important. By falling victim to materialism we are ignoring this truth. If we strive to deny the urge towards materialism then that is the intent we need to bring our hearts and minds into communion with the Divine. How much stuff do you have stored in your basement or attic? You could probably sell much of that and give that money to the poor without even noticing that the stuff is gone. Examine your life and the things you have accumulated around you. If you are like most of us in the west, you will likely find that you have much room for improvement in this area.

In essence, this comes down to the evaluation of the choices we make. We can choose to gratify the ego or to submit to something more transcendent. We can change what we value. As it says in the Mass: "Help us always to remember that material things are to be used, and people to be cherished; and that immorality is made manifest when people are used, and material things cherished." If we emphasize the value of people over things, we become attuned to the Sacred Flame as it is manifest in the people of the world. This includes consideration for the conditions of the people in poorer countries who work long hours in dreadful conditions to make the things that we covet. Look at the things in your home. Use this as an opportunity to ask questions about the values you have placed on your possessions.

We all need to own things, and this shouldn't be seen as a condemnation of your way of life. There are many ways to exist as a modern person acting spiritually in the world. Be aware of your choices. Donate money and objects to worthy charities, and by so doing, improve the lives of those around you. Remember the example of the Beloved Disciple and be a brother or sister to your fellow travelers.

Sexual Abstinence

As you probably know, the Johannite Church has no particular stance on celibacy, either for its clergy or the laity; but just like fasting or living simply, sexual abstinence can be a useful spiritual tool when used properly. In the Eastern Orthodox tradition married couples are expected to practice sexual abstinence during many parts of the liturgical calendar. It can be a powerful method of self-denial, but as with so many ascetic practices it can also become a hindrance.

There is a reason that lust is one of the seven "deadly" sins. In the Sethian version of the creation myth, the Demiurge sows the seeds of lust in the newly created humans in order to do two things: to generate more humans to worship him, and to give humans a distraction from spiritual matters. This works some of the time, but it also backfires most spectacularly in one particular instance in the story. Through a pure act of love, which mirrored the proper Divine order of the Pleroma, Adam and Eve bore a third son, Seth, who would be a kind of savior figure to the Sethian Gnostics. So to say that the ancient (or modern) Gnostics were simply world-hating dualists is only a very shallow understanding of a complex theology. As a result, for the ancient Gnostics, as for us today, sexuality has spiritual consequences both challenging and rewarding.

It's difficult to describe where one might draw the line today between good sex and bad sex (in a moral sense) but a good indicator is, like the other practices, intent. If we see sex in terms of a distraction from the spiritual life, then we can engage in it with that understanding and return to our spiritual pursuits afterwards. There are those who find the Divine to be present in sex. For some people, lust is a particular problem. For these perhaps an extended period of sexual abstinence would be useful, but for all of us, a more considered approach to sex with a Gnostic world view in mind would help tremendously.

Another aspect of lust is the sexual desire we

experience when we see or interact with a person we are attracted to physically. This is a natural part of being human, but it can also be a serious hindrance to spiritual development. Try, for a day, to really be aware of your thoughts and feelings in this regard. Recognize feelings of lust you experience for the people you see as you go about your day. Pay particular attention to the advertising you encounter. Ads are often designed to elicit lustful thoughts. Once you become aware that you are experiencing lust, think about how these feelings arose. Part of the source of those feelings is certainly our physical bodies, but quite a bit of it is also conditioned responses based on our cultural contexts. When we react to something without our conscious awareness, which happens nearly constantly, we are not living in an awareness of the Sacred Flame. By recognizing when this happens, we take another step towards the mastery of our unconscious minds, opening the door just a little bit wider to the influence of the Divine.

If you decide to practice sexual abstinence as part of your spiritual practice, be it for a short time or indefinitely, always remember that all ascetic practices can either serve the ego or the transcendent. If you approach celibacy with the intent to remove distractions, be sure that you don't let it become a badge of honor that shows the world how spiritual you are. You will find that the distractions caused by celibacy can be quite overwhelming. Prayer helps tremendously in this regard. Obviously, this is not a path that can be walked casually. However, those who persevere will find great benefit from a practice that includes sexual abstinence.

Retreats

While a lot of this book focuses on ways to add spiritual practices to your daily life, you may also wish to take time away from your daily life to focus on spiritual practices. This is called a retreat, and you can think of it as a spiritual vacation. Retreats help to recharge our spiritual batteries. The benefits of spending time apart from the world in retreat are numerous and wonderful.

Retreats can be directed or not, silent or not, for a weekend, a week, or even a whole month. A directed retreat is one that has a scheduled program, and there are many that are run by the more mainstream Christian denominations that would be very appropriate for a Johannite. There are retreats that are self-directed, which means you can choose what you do on the retreat. Some retreats are simply silent. No talking is allowed, except sometimes in your own room for prayers.

You can also make a retreat in your home. Take some time off from work, turn off your phone and computer and spend the time in prayer and contemplation. Make sure you won't be disturbed. If you don't have the luxury of spending whole days in retreat, you can also take a series of mini-retreats in the evenings for several days in a row. Any time spent in retreat, whether a 30 day silent intense retreat or a few hours in the evening, will be very valuable in fostering awareness of the Sacred Flame.

There are many places offering retreats that might be compatible with Johannite spirituality. You can find one near you on http://www.retreatfinder.com which has a rather large listing of retreat centers by location. You can also filter the list based on the type of retreat being offered. It is a very useful tool.

The Johannite Church has a Conclave each year, which is similar to a retreat, but aimed more at education and fellowship. These usually happen in May, and more information can be found on the AJC's website. Information about the next upcoming Conclave is usually posted after the first of the year.

Esoteric Orders

Another form of advanced spiritual work, requiring much personal commitment and self-motivation, is to join an esoteric order. If you are familiar with them at all, you probably already have an opinion about esoteric orders; it could be positive or it could be very negative. An esoteric order is simply another tool, and almost all esoteric orders[19] are working towards the good of humanity and the spiritual development of their members.

You may have heard some unpleasant things about esoteric orders. Rest assured, esoteric orders do not worship the devil, they worship the Divine. Esoteric orders are designed to help their initiates to grow in their relationship to the Divine and bring Divine Grace into the physical world. An initiate works to bring his or her psyche into alignment with the Divine Will, just like the

---

19 With some exceptions. There are those who try to take advantage of people both in the esoteric community as well as in the rest of the world. Because of their secret nature it can be difficult to tell if an order is on the up and up, so a conversation with a member of the Johannite clergy can be invaluable in picking the right one for you.

members of the Orthodox and Roman Catholic churches; they simply use a different set of tools to do it.

On the other hand, some people have a tendency to romanticize esoteric orders. This can be as problematic as demonizing them. Most esoteric lodge meetings in the modern world aren't made up of hundreds of robed figures meeting secretly in underground chambers decorated with secret symbols, performing rituals to change the directions of the tides of fate and influence world leaders. Most lodges are made up of a handful of regular people meeting in someone's living room having conversations about old books. Esoteric work is very hard work, and it is work on your own psyche first and foremost, which is long, boring, and often a bit upsetting. Working through emotional issues is very stressful, whether done in a ritual setting or in the office of a therapist.

It can also be very rewarding to the dedicated esotericist. Consistent practice of the techniques taught by esoteric orders can bypass the rulers of this world, the archons, negating their influence and bringing the true Will of the Divine into the world. The orders mentioned in this chapter are those that are very compatible with Johannite spirituality. Many of the clergy and laity of the Church are initiates of one or more of these orders.

Esoteric orders are, by definition, secret. It may seem odd, in this age of ubiquitous information, to keep secrets, however, they have their own value. Information that is handed over freely has no value, but information that is guarded and given only after hard work and accomplishment is very valuable indeed. That is the key to esoteric secrecy. Dion Fortune said it best in her book Sane Occultism:

"The true occult secrets have never been betrayed in their entirety. In fact, it is only the lesser secrets that are capable of betrayal; the higher secrets of the mystical consciousness are incapable of betrayal because they are not communicated, but realized."

Therefore, secrecy in esoteric work isn't there to keep "the profane" from learning the teachings of the order. Almost all of the "secrets" are available online anyway. The secrecy is part of the learning process.

If you are interested in more detailed information

about any of the orders in this chapter, links will be provided to their official websites, if such websites exist, or efforts will be made to point you in a direction that should lead the diligent seeker to more information.

The Friary/Ordo Sacrae Flammae

The Friary/OSF is very closely related to the Johannite Church. It was founded by Bishop Foster and the early modern Johannite community before the founding of the AJC, and its rituals and ceremonies are very closely aligned with those of the Church. They are, however, distinctly separate organizations, and membership in one has nothing to do with membership in the other. Esoterically inclined Johannites would find much value in the work of the Friary.

The Friary is different from many of the other orders in this chapter in one very significant way. It doesn't have much of a specific set of teachings; rather it relies on the initiate to learn in a self-directed way. New initiates are given the tools to learn the basics, but beyond that the learning is very self-directed. Initiates are expected to bring what they learn back to the Order and share it. In the more advanced grades, initiates conduct their own research into a subject of their choosing, almost like an esoteric doctoral thesis. Think of it as more of a laboratory than an esoteric order.

For the first two degrees an initiate needs to be closely mentored by a Friar of the second degree or higher. Because of this, the Friary chooses new members very carefully. The existing Friars already have a heavy workload, and we don't want to sacrifice the education of existing Friars just so we can take in new members. That shouldn't discourage the serious aspirant, however. Interest in the Johannite tradition and the willingness to purchase and read a book on the subject shows that you would be a good candidate. If you have decided that the Friary is a path you'd like to take, speaking with your local Johannite clergy-person is a good place to start. In the meantime you can find more information about the Friary on its website: http://johannite.org/friary.

Freemasonry

Freemasonry is one of the oldest continuing esoteric orders in the world today. The problem is that most Masons wouldn't call Masonry esoteric. Let me assure you that it is indeed. Those who designed Freemasonry many centuries ago were almost certainly Hermeticists, Rosicrucians, and Alchemists. Masonry is highly influenced by Egyptian and Greek mystery schools. All of these esoteric streams come together in Masonry, but most Masons think of it as more of a social club. The good news is, it can be both.

One of the most ingenious principles included in the founding framework of Freemasonry was the requirement of each member to memorize, word for word, the rituals of the Craft, as it is known. No innovation is allowed in the content of the ritual[20] so the esoteric secrets are still available to those with ears to hear. Esoterically inclined Masons will have to do some extra work to wring the truth from the rituals, but it's all there. Jules Doinel also

20 Though innovation has been constant since the first public Masonic meeting in 1717, wise hands have guided the changes.

made the claim that the true religion of Freemasonry is Gnosticism. This is not strictly true, as Masonry does not dictate its members to have any specific religion, but Gnostic religion does go quite well with the teachings of Freemasonry.

Freemasonry has traditionally only been available to men, but there are other types of Masonry available for both women and men, such as Co-Masonry, among others. Men will certainly have an easier time finding a Masonic lodge to join than women, which is unfortunate, but it's how Masonry has almost always been. There are certain rules one agrees to when becoming a Freemason, but they aren't anything you might find objectionable, generally. A quick internet search will turn up a great deal of information about joining the Masons. As with most organizations these days they are shrinking in membership and new members are almost always welcomed with open arms.

Martinism

What we know today as Martinism comes primarily from the teachings of two French gentlemen as viewed through the lens of another French gentleman some 100+ years after the first two gentlemen. It is a system of Christian mysticism and theurgy (ritual magical practice with the intent of unity with the Divine) concerned with the fall of the first man, his state of material privation from his Divine source, and the process of his return, called 'Reintegration' or illumination.

Martinez de Pasqually; Rosicrucian, Swedenborgian, Kabbalist, and scholar of ancient mystery religions, founded an order called "Ordre des Chevaliers Maçons Elus Cohens de l'Univers" (Order of Knight Masons, Elect Priests of the Universe) or, the "Elus Cohen" in the middle of the 18th century. This order focused mostly on theurgy, kabbalah, and alchemy, and its aim was to give initiates a set of rituals to conjure a spirit that would assist them in their initiation.

A few years after founding the Elus Choen, Pasqually initiated Louis Claude de Saint-Martin, a lawyer who joined the French army as an officer in order to have more free time to study esoteric books. Saint-Martin was more interested in a mystic's path than the theurgy taught by Pasqually, and he left the Elus Cohen to develop a system of his own which he would call "The Way of the Heart". However, his work was still heavily influenced by the teachings of Pasqually, and also the works of Jacob Boehme. Saint-Martin's theology is virtually identical to that of Boehme.

After a century or more of loosely affiliated independent students of The Way of the Heart working on their own and initiating new students, and the Elus Cohen fading into Masonic obscurity, Dr. Gerard Encausse, known also by the ecclesiastical name of Papus, formed the Martinist Order as a way of bringing the teachings of Pasqually and Saint-Martin together under one roof. He merged the teachings of Saint-Martin and the practices and lodge structure of Pasqually into something entirely new. He did all this in 1882[21] in a climate in France that was very conducive to esoteric work. In fact, it was around this same time that the Gnostic Church was being restored by Doinel, who would later confirm that Martinism is essentially Gnostic.

Various Martinist orders continue to exist to this day,

---

21 Various sources give many different dates, but for simplicity we'll assume 1882.

stemming from the order created by Papus, in addition to many independent Free Initiators, after the practice of Saint-Martin. This is a very brief overview. If you would like more information, I gave a talk on the history of Martinism[22] for the Occult of Personality podcast a few years ago, which may help with the details.

The work of Martinism is the reintegration of the individual with the unity of the Divine. It does this by teaching meditations and rituals that will help the initiate transcend his or her mundane personality and understand the essential unity of the universe and the Divine. The teachings of Martinism mirror some of the chivalric traditions, such as those of the Knights Templar, and it could be said to be a part of the secret Johannite tradition. Because of this, Johannites will find Martinism to be very compatible with their spirituality.

One way to learn more about joining a Martinist order would be to have a conversation with a member of the Johannite clergy. Not all of the clergy are Martinists, but they will all be able to point you in the right direction

22 http://www.occultofpersonality.net/membership/a-lecture-on-martinism

and help you connect with the Martinist tradition that is right for you.

Gnostic Voudon and Points Chaud

Our apostolic lineage travels through Haiti in the last part of the 19th and first part of the 20th centuries through a series of esoteric Freemasons and voudon practitioners. Gnosticism and Freemasonry have a long history together, and Gnosticism has enjoyed a safe haven in Haiti for many years among the voudon community. It is no wonder that the three traditions have become merged in Gnostic Voudon.

Gnostic Voudon was brought to the English speaking world by Tau[23] Michael Bertiaux primarily through his epic work The Voudon Gnostic Workbook. It is a lengthy book that covers a lot of esoteric ground. In more recent years parts of the Gnostic Voudon system developed by Bertiaux has been expanded and brought more into line with the esoteric Masonic tradition of Memphis and Misraim by Tau Allen Greenfield and others, referred to

---

23 Tau is a title used by Bishops in the French Gnostic tradition.

commonly as the Points Chaud[24] work. Greenfield participates in a non-hierarchical magical system called Congregational Illuminism which is the group that promulgates this version of the Points Chaud work.

The Points Chaud, as practiced in Gnostic Voudon, are points that correspond to areas of the physical body and to the 97 degrees of Memphis-Misraim Freemasonry. The points are activated by someone who has already activated that point on their own body. This activation serves as a mini initiation, an awakening to awareness of the Divine through both the activation itself and subsequent meditation upon that point.

Congregational Illuminists work this system both individually and in groups; there is no dictated structure. Indeed nothing about the Points work in the Congregational Illuminist tradition is dictated. As a result there are many different ways of working with the Points. Various groups and individuals working with this system each have their own process.

In reality, Gnostic Voudon and the Points Chaud work

---

24 French for "hot points" and ponounced "pwen show."

can't accurately be called Gnostic, Voudon, or Freemasonry; it is something else entirely. Traditional Haitian Voudon practitioners would not recognize it, there is no Gnostic cosmology to speak of, and there is no Freemasonry going on at all. All that being said, it has value for the Johannite to whom this sort of symbolism is appealing. To find out more about the Points work you can listen to interviews with Tau Greenfield on the Occult of Personality podcast at http://occultofpersonality.net

The Order of St. Esclarmonde

The Order of Saint Esclarmonde is a Gnostic, monastic lay Order open to women and men, sponsored by both the Gnostic Church of Mary Magdalene and the Apostolic Johannite Church. Novices are not required to be members of either church.

The purpose of the Order is to provide structure to committed, solitary, traditional spiritual practice. Nuns and Monks of the Order commit to mindfulness, daily contemplation, and community action through charitable works. This is a way to dedicate yourself to a regular Gnostic spiritual practice that is in communion with others from around the world who are doing the exact same practices. During daily prayer, nuns and monks wear the traditional white alb and white cincture as both a reminder of their connection to others undertaking this work, and as a symbol of purification.

Saint Esclarmonde was an early 13th century Cathar mystic. She is traditionally identified as the woman who successfully debated the virtues of Catharism against the founder of the Inquisition, St. Dominic. Legend has it that when the Inquisition finally came to take her to her execution, she turned into a dove and flew away. Her legend was romanticized during the Napoleonic era to the point where she became a kind of Cathar Joan of Arc and patroness of the revival of art and mysticism of the 19th century.

The Proctor for female novices is Reverend Mother Marsha Emrick of the GCMM, while male novices are Proctored by Monsignor Jordan Stratford of the AJC. If you are interested in learning more about the Order of St. Esclarmonde you can visit their page on the AJC website where you can also find the vows and application requirements. From there you can email Msgr. Stratford or Rev. Mother Emrick for more information or to submit your application.

Other Orders

There are many other esoteric orders available, some more closely aligned with the principles of the Johannite Church than others. A few deserve a passing mention, although these aren't as closely related to Gnosticism as the ones previously mentioned.

The Hermetic Order of the Golden Dawn was created in the late 19th century by a group of Freemasons who were looking for something more openly esoteric that also allowed women to join. They created the Golden Dawn under the guidance of a group of adepts known as the Secret Chiefs who taught the early group its rituals and teachings. The Golden Dawn practices theurgy, hermetics, Qabalah[25], and alchemy. Its symbols are Egyptian.

The Theosophical Society was formed in 1875 to advance the spiritual principles and search for Truth

---

25 Spelled this way to distinguish it from Jewish Kabbalah.

known as Theosophy. Theosophy teaches that there are many paths to the Divine and seeks to find the commonalities between those paths. Many Theosophical scholars have written extensively on Gnosticism, most notably G. R. S. Mead. The Theosophical Society is more of a school than an esoteric order, but membership in the Society has many advantages, including access to their libraries, which are often very well stocked with esoteric texts. The TS symbols are many, but they primarily focus on Tibetan Buddhist and Hindu symbolism.

Chapter 8: Next Steps

If you haven't already, the best thing to do next is to talk to some Johannites. Find the contact information for the closest Johannite community and send them an email. Ask questions, start a conversation, and get involved. "Like" the Johannite Church on Facebook and circle it on Google+, you can join in the conversation on the internet and there is an entire global community who can answer your questions. Also, read the Church's website and be sure you understand what it says. It's a great resource for those who are new to our traditions.

Visit a Parish

It can be a challenge to find a local Johannite group at this point in time. If you don't live near one, you can still visit one. See if you can schedule your next vacation in an area where there is a Johannite parish or narthex. Email the rector and let them know that you're coming. Visiting guests are always welcome. You can find a list of the Johannite bodies on the Church's website.

Attend Conclave

Each year the Johannite Church holds a Conclave, which is a retreat of sorts. It has historically been designed primarily for clergy, but much effort has been made in recent years to open up the program to the laity and provide things that they might find interesting. For a Johannite, attending a Conclave is a great way to see the Church in action - not to mention the fact that you'll meet many Johannites from all over the world. The Conclave is typically held towards the end of May, though circumstances may cause that to move around a bit. You can see information about the upcoming Conclave on the Church's website, depending on the time of year.

Join the Church

The Church has no formal membership requirements, and its sacraments are open to all. This means that you can attend a Johannite mass, take communion with everybody else, get married by a Johannite priest, and so on, and never officially become a member. You can, however, choose to become an official member of the church if you wish to show your commitment to the Johannite traditions. There is no set procedure for preparing to join the Church. It usually involves a conversation with a priest and a period of discernment. This period can be spent learning about the Church, its theology, history, and traditions to make sure you really want to be a part of our community.

Joining the Church also means taking extra responsibility for your own spiritual development. You will be encouraged to develop a serious religious practice and you will be expected to to be very diligent in recognizing when you sin, or miss the mark, and take steps to correct those actions or inactions. Being a Johannite means dedicating your life the the pursuit of Gnosis. Practice and awareness go hand in hand with this dedication.

Becoming a member of the Church also opens up more opportunities for leadership positions. There are many committees, Congregations, and Dicasteries that have lay members serving in them. To learn more or become an official member of the Johannite Church, contact your nearest priest or bishop.

Start a Narthex

The word narthex is an architectural term. It refers to

the front part of a church, before you enter the sanctuary. In the Church, as a description of a Johannite body, it is the first stage in the development of a local parish. It can stand alone as a lay led group that has no intention of becoming a parish, or it can be a distinct part of an existing parish. It is most often run by a lay person or a cleric in minor orders in preparation for the priesthood. The program at a narthex usually includes the Logos Service, a reading and discussion group, group meditation or contemplative practice, regular Agape Meals, and much more.

Starting a narthex is a labor of love. Most narthexes are started by people who want to belong to a Gnostic community, but there is no such community in their area. It can also be frustrating, as it can take quite a long time before people start to show up with any regularity. If you decide to take this path, the best advice is to stick with it through the difficult times. Almost every parish of the AJC started out as a narthex, and it can be done if the leader is persistent.

Starting a narthex is a longer process, simply because the leader of the narthex is an official representative of the Church and is required to be a member of the church. An application is also submitted to be a narthex leader, which involves a number of essays and a background check. Inquiries can be made to the Executive Assistant to the Patriarch, whose email can be found on the Johannite website.

Holy Orders

The Independent Sacramental Movement as a whole, and ecclesiastical Gnosticism in particular, usually attracts a much smaller percentage of casual attendees than the larger, more mainstream faiths. Most people who come to Gnosticism do so by jumping in with both feet. This is understandable. Those of us who identify as Gnostic probably spent a long time reading about Gnosticism by themselves, and upon finding a group of like-minded people with whom they can share their love of all things Gnostic, the enthusiasm is hard to contain. As a result, many Gnostics feel a desire to be as involved as they can in their chosen community. In the case of the AJC, this often means ordination into Holy Orders.

There are ten Holy Orders in the Johannite Church,

five Minor Orders and five Major Orders. The Minor Orders are; Cleric, Doorkeeper, Reader, Exorcist, and Acolyte. The Major Orders are; Subdeacon, Deacon, Priest, Bishop, and Patriarch. Each Holy Order has a very specific function, and one does not need to have a desire to become a priest to enter into formation for Holy Orders. If one particular Order speaks to you, then there is nothing preventing you from becoming ordained to that Order and going no further. Orders must be conferred in order, so, for example, one does not become a Reader without first becoming a Cleric, followed by Doorkeeper.

A Cleric is someone who has dedicated themselves in service to the community of the Church. Generally, in practice, this means that a Cleric assists the other members of the clergy in their sacramental functions. They can help set up for the mass or other parish functions, assist in the day-to-day operations of a parish or diocese, or perform other functions as needed by the ecclesiastical hierarchy. When one enters into the Minor Orders, one is also expected to develop practices that will enhance their spiritual development. In the case of the Cleric, he or she is expected to exercise self-control with regard to the physical body as the temple for the Spirit.

A Doorkeeper arrives early for Mass to open the doors and prepare the space. The role of the Doorkeeper is to prepare, both internally and in the physical world, for the coming of the Logos in the Eucharist. The Doorkeeper also continues the spiritual work begun while he/she was a Cleric, opening and clearing the way for further spiritual development. The spiritual work of the Doorkeeper is to transform the emotions and passions to the service of the Divine.

The primary role of the Reader is to read the First Reading during the Mass. However, a Reader will also make a special effort to read as much as possible outside of the Liturgy as well. This is an Order that is primarily concerned with the intellect. Training of the intellect and concentration are the most important tasks of the Reader.

The Exorsist, in this case, is not the exorcist priest like you see in the movies. The exorcism of spirits and demons has its place, but this is not the Order that does that particular work. This Order focuses on healing, both for themselves and for the people. In order to do this, the

Exorcist must be in control of his or her Will. This is a process that is extensively discussed in esoteric schools and literature. The work of this Order is truly challenging, but extremely important for the life of the Church.

The primary functions of the Acolyte are to assist at the altar during the Mass and light the candles. The inner work of the Acolyte is to purify the ego and remove themselves from the gravitational pull of egocentricity. Freedom from attachments is also the goal of the practices in this book. An Acolyte will find themselves spending a great deal of time using some of the practices you've learned here.

The Major Orders are much more involved. Becoming a Deacon or Priest is a challenging and rewarding process for those who are called to it. It's a life dedicated to service, and, quite frankly, it's often very disruptive to one's personal life. The priesthood formation program of the church takes a minimum of four years to complete and there will be some travel involved, as you will be required to attend the annual Conclave and other events. A priest has a responsibility to see to the spiritual wellbeing of the members of his/her parish and beyond. A

Johannite priest is a facilitator, helping the laity and clergy in the parish develop the tools to attain to Gnosis. It's no small task, but there are many people in the Church who will help. Nobody is in this alone.

If you are considering Holy Orders, please contact a member of the clergy and he or she can help you to explore your options. If, after a period of prayer and discernment you feel called to this life of service to the Johannite community, you can visit the AJC's website to read about vocations. Instructions for how to apply are available there.

Conclusion

It is my hope that this book has given you more than a few ideas to get you started on your personal practice. Every practice presented here is deserving of its own book, and most of them do, in fact, have volumes dedicated to their study. If you find yourself drawn to one or more of the practices introduced in this book I would highly encourage you to do more research. Find a teacher, if you can, who specializes in your chosen practice. There is no substitute for the tutelage of an experienced teacher.

Most importantly, just start. Even if you aren't doing the practice exactly right, the intent to do it is the key. Start today. Decide on a schedule and stick to it. You won't always remember to do your practice, especially at first. Don't beat yourself up, that's part of being human. Developing a new habit requires the re-wiring of your brain, little by little, over time. Every time you remember that you forgot that is a step in the right direction; it reinforces the new patterns and you have a chance to make a little more progress. It's incremental, so treat it that way and you can't help but be successful in the long run.

And finally, if you have any questions about the practices, or about the Johannite Church in general, please don't hesitate to ask. Send me an email any time and I would be happy to help. I wish you all the best on your spiritual journey.

Yours Before the Sacred Flame,

Fr. Anthony Silvia

Appendix

The Liturgical Calendar of the Apostolic Johannite Church

New Year's Day: January 1

Epiphany: January 6

Candlemas Day: February 2

Holy Valentinus: February 14

Bernard-Raymond Fabre Palaprat: February 18

Ash Wednesday: Moveable[26]

Holy Pelagius: March 6

Montesegur Day: March 16

Jacques de Molay: March 18

Martyrdom of Tau Harmonius: March 22

Holy Archangel Gabriel: March 24

The Annunciation of Our Lady: March 25

Palm Sunday: Moveable

Maundy Thursday:Moveable

Good Friday: Moveable

Holy Saturday: Moveable

Easter Sunday: Moveable

Holy Apostles, Philip and James: May 1

---

26 Moveable feasts follow the conventions of the Roman
    Catholic liturgical calendar.

St. Julian of Norwich: May 8

Holy Apostle Matthias: May 14

Ascension Day: Moveable

Pentecost: Moveable

Trinity Sunday: Moveable

Corpus Christi: Moveable

St. Sarah the Egyptian: May 24

St. Joan of Arc: May 30

Holy Columba: June 9

Holy Apostle Barnabas: June 11

Holy Archangel Uriel: June 21

The Nativity of St. John the Baptist: June 24

Holy Apostles Peter and Paul: June 29

Holy Mary Magdalene: July 22

Holy Apostle James: July 25

Holy Joseph of Arimathea/ Lammas: July 31

Transfiguration of the Lord: August 6

The Assumption of the Holy Sophia: August 15

Holy Abbot Bernard of Clairvaux: August 20

Holy Apostle Bartholomew: August 24

The Descent of the Holy Sophia: September 8

Hildegard of Bingen: September 17

Holy Apostle Matthew: September 21

Restoration Day: September 22

Holy Archangel Michael: September 29

Holy Francis of Assisi: October 4

Martyrdom of the Holy Templars: October 13

St. Teresa of Avila: October 16

Holy St. James the Just: October 23

Holy Apostles Simon & Jude: October 28

All Saints Day: November 1

All Soul's Day: November 2

Gregory Palamas: November 14

All Gnostic Saints: November 22

Holy Apostle Andrew: November 30

Advent Sunday: Moveable

Holy St. Nicholas: December 6

Holy Apostle Thomas: December 21

Holy Archangel Raphael: December 22

Nativity of the Divine Light: Christmas Day: December 25

Holy Apostle John, the Beloved: December 27

Recommended Reading

Of course, Gnostics value knowledge quite highly. Here are some books that are invaluable to a modern Gnostic. There has been much progress in the study of Gnosticism in recent years, and these represent some of the best. Also, there are books here that will help you learn more about the practices introduced in the book. These are just a beginning, though. There are enough books on the subject to keep you busy for the rest of your life, just don't forget to find time for practice.

Johannite History and Traditions

The Community of the Beloved Disciple: The Life, Loves and Hates of an Individual Church in New Testament Times - Raymond Edward Brown

Living Gnosticism: An Ancient Way of Knowing - Jordan Stratford

The Levitikon - Translated by Donald Donato

The Secret Revelation of John - Karen L. King

Gnosticism & Hermeticism

The Gnostics: History*Tradition*Scriptures*Influence - Andrew Phillip Smith

The Gnostic Bible: Revised and Expanded Edition - Edited by Willis Barnstone & Marvin Meyer

Hermetica, Vol. 1: The Ancient Greek and Latin Writings Which Contain Religious or Philosophic Teachings Ascribed to Hermes Trismegistus - Translated by Walter Scott

The Kybalion - Three Initiates

Meditation

Sadhana: A Way to God - Anthony de Mello

Raja-Yoga - Swami Vivekananda

Spiritual Direction and Meditation - Thomas Merton

Compassion and Meditation: The Spiritual Dynamic between Buddhism and Christianity - Jean-Yves Leloup

Meditation for Beginners - Jack Kornfield

Christian Contemplation

Finding Grace at the Center: The Beginning of Centering Prayer - M. Basil Pennington, Thomas Keating, Thomas E. Clarke

Centering Prayer and Inner Awakening - Cynthia Bourgeault

The Wisdom Jesus: Transforming Heart and Mind--A New Perspective on Christ and His Message - Cynthia Bourgeault

The Wisdom Way of Knowing: Reclaiming An Ancient Tradition to Awaken the Heart - Cynthia Bourgeault

The Way of a Pilgrim and The Pilgrim Continues His Way - Translated by Olga Savin

Esoteric Orders

Inside a Magical Lodge: Group Ritual in the Western Tradition - John Michael Greer

Esoteric Orders and Their Work - Dion Fortune

The Western Esoteric Traditions: A Historical Introduction - Nicholas Goodrick-Clarke

The Golden Thread: The Ageless Wisdom of the Western Mystery Traditions - Joscelyn Godwin

Born in Blood: The Lost Secrets of Freemasonry - John J. Robinson

About the Author

 Fr. Anthony Silvia is a priest of the Apostolic Johannite Church, an experienced nonprofit administrator, and a lover of the esoteric and the arcane. Fr. Silvia is the Rector of Saint Martin's Parish, in New York City, and has been successful in growing the Johannite Church wherever he has been. He is a Martinist, a Freemason, and a member of The Friary/Order of the Sacred Flame and has studied esoteric orders and their works for many years. He enjoys singing in the barbershop harmony style, Steampunk, and starting interesting projects.

Author photo by Thomas Langley

Cover photo by Carl Silvia

4185707R00128

Printed in Great Britain
by Amazon.co.uk, Ltd.,
Marston Gate.